Anglican Spirituality

"What does it mean to be spiritual in an Anglican way? How can we get closer to God so that we pulse with the life of Christ? This book answers those questions in ways that are both deep and accessible. Fr Greg Peters is one of Anglican theology's best, especially on this subject. I recommend this book to all clergy and serious parishioners, particularly for adult study groups."

—**GERALD MCDERMOTT**, author of *Deep Anglicanism*

"'There is no Anglicanism apart from the Book of Common Prayer,' writes Dr. Peters in his introduction. This statement sums up what many of us believe—and yet, you can find some Anglicans who rarely, if ever, use the prayer book. This brief introduction to Anglican spirituality ought to convince every English-speaking Christian of what a treasure the prayer book is. It is our Rule of Life. It is a tried-and-true way of reading and praying Holy Scripture in a formative way. I pray that this book will be used by God to convince every person in our tradition of this truth, and that it may also convince newcomers to the Anglican way of the same."

—**CHARLES F. CAMLIN**, dean, Cranmer Theological House

"Students of the Anglican Way will be nurtured by the symphonic blend of doxology, theology, and ecclesiology as they read *Anglican Spirituality: An Introduction*. The Rev. Dr. Greg Peters effectively explains how the Anglican Book of Common Prayer's application of the threefold Benedictine Rule—Daily Office, Holy Communion, private devotion—systematically advances spirituality through the daily corporate and individual reading of the Bible and prayers."

—**STEVEN RICHARD RUTT**, associate professor of biblical studies, Arizona Christian University

"Fr. Greg Peters, in this simple book, *Anglican Spirituality*, has captured the fundamental heart of Anglican Spirituality. Fr. Peters captures the Anglican distinctive that our relationship with Christ is not simply 'me and Jesus' but it is Jesus, His Church and His people of which each individual is a vital component as St. Paul describes in 1st Corinthians 12:15ff. Thus, Fr. Peters lays out the classic Anglican form—Gather, Praise, Receive, and Give. I will be recommending this book to my clergy and all the people of the Anglican Diocese of San Joaquin."

—**ERIC VAWTER MENEES**, bishop ordinary,
Anglican Diocese of San Joaquin

Anglican Spirituality

An Introduction

Greg Peters

Foreword by Ray Sutton

CASCADE *Books* • Eugene, Oregon

ANGLICAN SPIRITUALITY
An Introduction

Cascade Books
An Imprint of Wipf and Stock Publishers
199 W. 8th Ave., Suite 3
Eugene, OR 97401

www.wipfandstock.com

PAPERBACK ISBN: 979-8-3852-1130-2
HARDCOVER ISBN: 979-8-3852-1131-9
EBOOK ISBN: 979-8-3852-1132-6

Cataloguing-in-Publication data:

Names: Peters, Greg, 1971– [author]. | Sutton, Ray R., 1950– [foreword writer].

Title: Anglican spirituality : an introduction / by Greg Peters.

Description: Eugene, OR: Cascade Books, 2024 | Includes bibliographical references and index.

Identifiers: ISBN 979-8-3852-1130-2 (paperback) | ISBN 979-8-3852-1131-9 (hardcover) | ISBN 979-8-3852-1132-6 (ebook)

Subjects: LCSH: Spiritual life—Anglican Communion. | Anglican Communion—Doctrines. | Spirituality—History. | Anglican Communion—History. | Anglican Communion.

Classification: BX5990 P48 2024 (paperback) | BX5990 (ebook)

VERSION NUMBER 03/18/25

To my former students and parishioners
who are now Anglican priests:

Frs. Nathan Warn, Matt Rucker, Wale Giwa, and Micah Hogan

Contents

Foreword

WHAT CHRISTIAN DOES NOT want to be spiritual? For a follower of Jesus Christ, the word "spiritual" means *godly* or *pious*. In fact, the old word for spirituality was piety. In many ways I prefer it. The word spirituality nowadays gets tossed around about everything from trees to hiking. Not for the Christian though. Spirituality is about godliness.

But that raises the further question, "How does a believer in Jesus Christ become godly . . . pious . . . spiritual?" Unfortunately, there is much vagueness even out there in God's kingdom. Sure, most Christians would agree that to be godly one needs to read the Scriptures. Of course there is prayer. And yes, a godly person needs to witness. Then sometimes a diligent soul will mention the other "w" word—worship.

Honestly, even much of the Christian literature sounds like how my grandmother used to describe what went into her amazing pecan pies at Thanksgiving. We called her Grandma Woosley; that was her last name. After an indulgent meal, we would gather around her chair and ask, "So what'd you put in your pie to make it so delicious?" Her response was always, "Oh, a little of this, and a little of that." We would laugh and repeat the same litany of question/response year after year. Unfortunately, that is how a lot of Christians approach the critically important topic of spirituality.

Thankfully, the Rev. Dr. Greg Peters has cut through the fuzzy shadows often circling around the word "spirituality." In his invaluable book, *Anglian Spirituality: An Introduction*, he draws on his own past scholarly research in monasticism. By it, he leads the reader to a definition of spirituality from his own tradition—Anglicanism. The combination of these lenses—monasticism and the Anglican Way—magnifies the essential ingredients of true spirituality. It is more than a "little of this and a little of that."

At one level Peters's book brings to us the driving center of the meaning of spirituality in monasticism. It is not so much that Peters explains it in his book. But it is there, behind what shapes his insights, and is therefore helpful to state. It is the monastic principle of biblical *simplicity* to follow Jesus Christ. Not in the sense of simpleton, shallow, or easy. Christlike simplicity is anything but those understandings of the word.

Jesus called his disciples away from the layers of clutter in their lives and culture that kept them from following the one true God. In the end, to keep total loyalty to their Lord and Master they were led to forfeit their lives for him. The height of the simplicity of being spiritual to become a martyr was, and is, seeing Jesus Christ (the *beatific vision*) amid true suffering. And it is not a kind of torture because of one's own odd personality or "screw ups." It is about beholding Christ at all personal costs at the most challenging moments of life to believe in and obey him and his Word.

It is a simple way of life in that it does not take a PhD to figure it out. It is not so simple, however, in doing what Scripture calls "suffering for righteousness' sake." That is the principle of simplicity in its most pristine form to which all monastic movements remind and help the church to be spiritual in the simplicity of Jesus. After all, he is the model. He gave up everything, even sitting at the right hand of God the Father, to become a man, suffer an agonizing passion, and die on a cross to pay for the sins of the world that we might gain the eternal life of the world to come. His mystical, though costly, life of simplicity, as articulated by monasticism in general, sets us up to understand Peters's approach to spirituality.

Pushing to another insight of monastic simplicity leading to spirituality, Peters clearly brings to the fore in his book the most influential of all the monastic movements in the person of Benedict of Nursia to provide a further definition of spirituality. A fifth-century Italian monk, Benedict founded twelve monastic communities. All monastic movements have what is called a "rule," their understanding of the path necessary for being spiritual. Benedict codified his *Rule* (*Regula*) into a book by that name.

Benedict's *Rule* centered on worship. He saw that Christ made disciples to do what God made humans to do from the beginning—worship him. And out of this worship would come a personal encounter with God's real presence to take the disciple into the world to be a witness for Christ and his good news, the gospel. But the profound principle of simplicity about worship for Benedict was that it was not just done on Sundays.

For Benedict, worship is threefold. It is the model of spirituality found in the emerging life of the church after Pentecost. Recorded in the book of Acts, it is weekly by means of the Eucharistic worship of God's people (Acts 20:7). It is also daily by observing hours of prayer, especially at the beginning and end of the day to replace the times of sacrifice in the temple (Acts 10:2–3). In addition, worship is by means of personal daily devotions, such as reading Scripture and praying privately. We see this third type of worship in the life of the Ethiopian Eunuch (Acts 8:26–40), who came to Christ during his devotional time when a deacon named Philip came across him while the Ethiopian was reading the book of Isaiah in the Bible.

Voila! Benedict translates the simplicity revealed in Holy Scripture about threefold worship into the *rule* of the monastic life of Benedictine monks. He enforces into daily routine private devotion, daily corporate prayer, and weekly Eucharist in the monastery. All this worship involved a rigorous reading of Scripture, prayer, and communion with Christ, both through daily personal devotion, getting low every day before God in petition and praise with the other monks, and Sunday worship together at the Eucharist.

Peters uses the larger and specific context of monasticism of Benedict to shape what is the concentration of his work, the Anglican Way of spirituality. This model of spirituality is expressed in the Book of Common Prayer. This book of worship puts in one place Benedict's *regula*. Reflecting the monk's insight, the Book of Common Prayer has three main services: daily Morning and Evening Prayer, weekly Holy Communion (though it can be done more often, on Saints' Days, for example), and Family Prayer for private devotion each day. There are other services such as Baptism, Confirmation, Ordination, and so forth. But the main ones are Benedict's threefold rule of worship.

Peters utilizes the insight and work of the important Anglican theologian Martin Thornton (d. 1986) to explain how a threefold kind of worship informs and forms true spirituality. One of Thornton's images of it is a fence. The main posts are weekly Eucharists. Smaller posts in between are like daily morning and evening prayer. And the long horizontal boards running across all the posts is private devotion. Thornton even said that this threefold rule was the way, like a fence, to keep the devil out of one's life.

Another voila! Peters uses the monastic guide of Benedict brought into the Anglican Book of Common Prayer to present many specifics about Anglican spirituality. He talks about an ancient way of reading and studying the Scriptures. He dissects the elements of prayer essential for the spiritual life. He even discusses the witness for the gospel that emerges from threefold worship. Hardly anywhere, if ever, is witness tied to spirituality. Peters does this because the Scriptures and the worship of the Book of Common Prayer do too.

In the end, Peters pulls what can be a fuzziness surrounding the topic of spirituality into clear definition. Therefore, it is with deep appreciation for what my good friend has accomplished that

I heartily commend his book. I promise that you will come away with more than "a little of this and a little of that."

The Most Rev. Dr. Ray R. Sutton
Presiding Bishop of the Reformed Episcopal Church
Dean and Ecumenical Dean
of the Anglican Church in North America

March 25, 2024
Feast of the Annunciation of the Blessed Virgin Mary

Preface

THIS BOOK ORIGINATED IN a series of lectures given at the Church of the Holy Communion Cathedral (Dallas, TX) for the One Hundred Fifteenth Synod of the Diocese of Mid-America, Reformed Episcopal Church, which is my own diocese. When Bp. Ray Sutton invited me to give these talks, he asked for the focus to be on "Anglican spirituality." As you will read below, there is not always clarity on either the meaning of "Anglican" or "spirituality." But I was confident that I would have something to say, even if it was not terribly original. It is common in Anglicanism to think of spirituality in relationship to the threefold rule of Daily Office, Holy Eucharist, and Private Devotion. Each of these areas of spirituality is guided by the Book of Common Prayer (BCP), for there is no Anglicanism apart from the BCP. Anglicans are a people of the books, if you will. This was made explicit by Thomas Cranmer (d. 1556) in the "Preface" to the BCP 1549: "Furthermore by this order [set out in the BCP], the curates shall need none other books for their public service, but this book and the Bible." Anglicans are nurtured and formed by the Holy Scriptures; thus, Anglicanism has a Scripture-based spirituality or expression of the faith. But Anglicans are also nurtured and formed by the BCP, so it is proper to say that Anglicanism has a prayer-book spirituality as well. And this is useful, reasonable, and entirely in keeping with Anglican polity and practice over the past five centuries. When Cranmer compiled, composed, and constructed the first BCP, he intended that it be used daily, weekly, and yearly. It was (and is), in many ways, a formational text. To be Anglican was, therefore, to be a BCP Anglican Christian as much as it was to be a biblical Anglican Christian.

Alongside the Sacred Scriptures, Anglican faith and practice also places great importance on the Holy Eucharist, which is *the* central work of the Church of Jesus Christ: "For as *often* as you eat this bread and drink the cup, you proclaim the Lord's death until he comes" (1 Cor 11:26).[1] This centrality is obvious when one simply looks at the contents of the first BCP from 1549. The "Preface" is followed by the "Table and Kalendar for Psalmes and Lessons [*sic*]," which is then followed by the Daily Office that makes use of the "Table and Kalender." This is followed straightaway by those elements necessary to the celebration of the Holy Eucharist: "Introites, Collectes, Epistles and Gospelles, to be used at the celebracion of the lordes Supper and holy Communion through the yere, with proper Psalmes and Lessons, for diverse feastes and days [*sic*]." This is followed by "The Supper of the Lorde and holy Communion, commonly called the Masse [*sic*]." The Daily Office is directly followed by the Holy Eucharist, like the threefold rule of Anglican spirituality.

Undergirding both the Daily Office and the Holy Eucharist is the preparatory and resulting work accomplished through individual personal devotion, characterized by such activities as fasting, studying, etc. Anglicanism has been open to the riches of the Christian tradition's variety of spiritual disciplines, saying little of what *ought* to be done but encouraging a wide array of activities for a host of reasons. There is a spirit of openness to what one thinks is good and right for oneself, as a complement to the expectation of faithful recitation of the Daily Office and frequent Holy Communion. All

---

1. Unless otherwise noted, all biblical citations are from the English Standard Version (ESV); italics added for emphasis. See Hardy, "Centrality of the Holy Eucharist"; and McDermott, "Centrality of the Eucharist."

Anglicans *ought* to pray the Daily Office and commune regularly, but only some should engage in other, particular spiritual practices.

With this threefold rule in mind, this book, after an introduction that helps define and describe "Anglican spirituality," will examine the place of the Daily Office, Holy Eucharist, and personal devotion in Anglican spirituality. The last chapter was written to help demonstrate that these practices are not impractical disciplines but form the very backbone of a properly *Anglican* theology of mission. Lastly, there is an appendix that uses one poem of John Donne (d. 1631) to lay out a theology of Anglican anthropology. The reader unfamiliar with theological anthropology might want to read this appendix first. Because all spirituality is rooted in a vision of what it means to be human, this appendix is intended to serve as a complement to the other chapters. The reader should keep in mind that the subtitle of this book is "An Introduction." It is *not* an exhaustive historical or theological presentation of "Anglican spirituality." It is meant to introduce the topic, without being overly superficial or simplistic. Its length is intentional, for it is an introduction, meant only to introduce the reader to the topic. It is aimed at all Anglican Christians, whether young or mature in their Anglican faith.

The greater part of this book was written in the Divinity Library of the University of Cambridge. Access to such an amenable environment is made possible by the Von Hügel Institute, St. Edmund's College, where I am a research associate. I am thankful to Dr. Vittorio Montemaggi, director of the Von Hügel Institute, and to its staff for their support during my stay, as well as the staff of the Divinity Faculty Library. I would also like to thank Bp. Ray Sutton for his invitation to deliver the initial talks and for writing the foreword. The ongoing support of my wife, Christina; sons, Brendan and Nathanael; daughter-in-law, Adri; and the parish of the Anglican Church of the Epiphany, La Mirada, California, continues to be invaluable in pursuing both my writing and priestly vocations. A final thank you is due to Robin Parry, my always supportive and encouraging editor at Wipf and Stock.

This book is dedicated to four priests who are also friends: Nathan Warn, Matt Rucker, Wale Giwa, and Micah Hogan. I had the good fortune of teaching each of these men during their journey to Anglican priesthood, hopefully saying helpful things. Their dedication and service to the church of Jesus Christ—as hospital chaplain, parish priest, and military chaplain—brings me deep delight.

I

Introduction

Defining Terms
What do we mean by "spirituality"?

THIS IS A BOOK on Anglican spirituality and like every book with the word "spirituality" in its title, it needs a word of explanation. The concept of "spirituality" is not a new one but it is one that in the modern era tends only to be used in conjunction with an adjective: medieval spirituality, Jesuit spirituality, Hindu spirituality, etc. The English word "spirituality" comes from the Latin *spiritualitas*, which is associated with the adjective *spiritualis* (spiritual) and these derive from the Greek noun *pneuma* (spirit) and the adjective *pneumatikos* (spiritual), which are not the opposite of "physical" or "material" (Greek *soma*, Latin *corpus*) but of "flesh" (Greek *sarx*, Latin *caro*) in the sense of those things that are contrary to the Spirit of God.[1] In the Latin Vulgate *spiritualis* translates the Greek *pneumatikos*, appearing twenty-two times. It was only in the fifth century that we find the first use of the

---

1. Sheldrake, *A Brief History*, 3.

1

noun *spiritualitas*, though it is still being used in the same way as *pneumatikos*, carrying the connotation of increasing one's hold on the Holy Spirit of Jesus, the source of the Christian life.[2] Over the course of the next 1,500 years the word (and concept) "spirituality" underwent significant development so that it came to mean, in general, "the deepest values and meanings by which people seek to live," implying "some kind of vision of the human spirit and of what will assist it to achieve full potential."[3] As Philip Sheldrake notes, "In Christian terms, spirituality refers to the way our fundamental values, lifestyles, and spiritual practices reflect particular understandings of God, human identity, and the material world as the context for human transformation." And, while "all Christian spiritual traditions are rooted in the Hebrew and Christian scriptures and particularly the gospels," they "are also attempts to reinterpret these scriptural values for specific historical and cultural circumstances."[4] Thus, "Anglican spirituality" is a uniquely Anglican endeavor to explain how baptized men and women seek to live out their lives over against the "flesh" in light of their understanding of the Christian Scriptures.

What do we mean by "Anglican"?

But this brings us to another point of definition, which is almost as rich in its history as "spirituality": what do I mean by "Anglican"?[5] "Anglican" and "Anglicanism" derive from the Latin word *anglicanus*, which means "English." Though the language of *ecclesia Anglicana* was used in the medieval church to refer to the church *in* England, the Magna Carta of 1215 spoke of the "English church" (*Anglicana ecclesia*), or, to quote the Act of Supremacy from 1534,

2. Bernard McGinn, "The Letter and the Spirit: Spirituality as an Academic Discipline," in Dreyer and Burrows, eds., *Minding the Spirit*, 26.

3. Sheldrake, *A Brief History*, 1–2.

4. Sheldrake, *A Brief History*, 7.

5. What follows is dependent on Paul Avis, "What Is 'Anglicanism'?," and J. Robert Wright, "Anglicanism, *Ecclesia Anglicana*, and Anglican: An Essay on Terminology," in Sykes and Booty, eds., *Study of Anglicanism*, 18–38, 406–24.

the king is "the only supreme head in earth of the Church of England called *Anglicana Ecclesia*." This gave the sixteenth-century English Reformers sufficient fodder to emphasize continuity with the early church and, thus, the English church's independence from papal jurisdiction. By the eighteenth century "Anglican" referred to a distinct theological position. For example, the writings of Edmund Burke (d. 1797) tell of the "Catholicks, Anglicans [and] Calvinists."

Apart from its historical genesis as a church in/of England, theologian Paul Avis speaks of an "Anglican Synthesis," which gets to the heart of what Anglicanism *is* versus where and when it originated. In a report drafted by the Archbishop of Canterbury William Temple (d. 1944) and submitted to the Lambeth Conference of 1930, we read,

> Our special characteristic and, as we believe, our peculiar contribution to the universal Church, arises from the fact that, owing to historic circumstances, we have been enabled to combine in our one fellowship the traditional faith and order of the Catholic Church with that immediacy of approach to God through Christ to which the evangelical churches especially bear witness, and freedom of intellectual enquiry, whereby the correlation of the Christian revelation and advancing knowledge is constantly effected.

Similarly, Archbishop of Canterbury Michael Ramsey (d. 1988), writing to a Roman Catholic audience, said,

> Our church has two aspects. . . . On the one hand we claim to be a church possessing Catholic tradition and continuity from the ancient Church, and our Catholic tradition and continuity includes the belief in the real presence of Christ in the Blessed Sacrament; the order of episcopacy and priesthood, including the power of priestly absolution. We possess various institutions belonging to Catholic Christendom like monastic orders for men and women. . . . Our Anglican tradition has another aspect as well. We are a church which has been through the Reformation, and values many experiences derived from the Reformation, for instance the open

> Bible: great importance is attached to the authority of the holy Scriptures, and to personal conviction and conversion through the work of the Holy Spirit.[6]

Notice several important items that define what it means to be an Anglican: (1) Anglicans practice "the traditional faith and order of the Catholic [i.e., universal] Church" for they are part of the "Catholic tradition" and in "continuity" with "the ancient Church," including "belief in the real presence of Christ in the Blessed Sacrament"; and (2) Anglicans hold to an "immediacy of approach to God through Christ" by means of "the open Bible" and "the work of the Holy Spirit." In short, "Anglican" means rooted in the Catholic faith and tradition while also valuing the Holy Scriptures and the work of the Holy Spirit in our lives. Thus, an *Anglican* spirituality will value these foci, it is this that makes Anglican spirituality particularly Anglican. To examine this uniquely Anglican spirituality, I am going to take my overall structure from the Book of Common Prayer (BCP).

The Threefold Vision of Anglican Spirituality

The prayer book lays out a Trinitarian, threefold vision of Anglican spirituality: Daily Office, Holy Eucharist, and private devotion (including private prayer). Ranging through each of these are the concepts of asceticism, union with God, and grace, for example. The venerable Anglican pastoral theologian Martin Thornton (d. 1986) wrote that the

> Rule of the Anglican Church can be summarized as consisting of (1) *the Office*, which is the corporate worship of the Body of Christ to the Father . . . (2) *The Mass* is the loving embrace of Christ in joy, attained by the synthesis of his complete succor offered and his absolute demand accepted . . . [and] (3) *Private prayer* concerns the sanctification of the individual soul by the indwelling spirit, to the glory of God.[7]

6. Both are cited in Avis, *Identity of Anglicanism*, 27–28.
7. Thornton, *Pastoral Theology*, 205–6.

Thornton goes on to note several benefits of this threefold Rule: it is a combination of both variable and invariable practices; it has a subjective–objective balance alongside an immanent–transcendent balance and an individual–corporate balance.

Before moving to this threefold vision of Anglican spirituality, let us unpack Thornton's benefits, as a way to delineate the larger contours of spirituality from an Anglican perspective.

Balance in Anglican Spirituality
The subjective–objective balance

First, the subjective–objective balance. There has always been a tension in the Jewish and subsequent Christian tradition between subjectivity and objectivity. Let us recall that God approached Abram as an individual with a request that he be father of a nation: "Now the LORD said to Abram, 'Go from your country and your kindred and your father's house to the land that I will show you. And I will make of you a great nation, and I will bless you and make your name great, so that you will be a blessing. I will bless those who bless you, and him who dishonors you I will curse, and in you all the families of the earth shall be blessed'" (Gen 12:1–3). Notice the use of "you" and "your" (ten times), which gets at the subjective nature of God's request. I am asking *you* Abram (the subjective) to leave so that *I* (the objective) can bless you and bless the nations through your offspring (cf. Gal 3:16). Or, to put in the conditional: *if* you leave, *then* I will bless you and others. God is not coercing Abram but allowing him to make an individual, subjective decision that will lead to the objective reality of God blessing him and blessing others through the people of God—the Jews. This subjective–objective nature of things continued into the New Testament era. For example, when Christ called the disciples, he was calling individual men (e.g., Peter and Andrew) to himself (Matt 4:19, "Follow me") but they had to leave their nets and follow him (Matt 4:20) so that they could "Go . . . and make disciples of all nations" (Matt 28:19).

A final example, theological in nature, touches on an important area of Anglican spirituality: the Holy Eucharist. When the church offers the Eucharist to her members, it is with the understanding that there is both a subjective and objective reality to the sacrament. According to the BCP, the worthy reception of Christ's body and blood follows, in part, from a genuine confession of sin wherein the penitent fully intends amendment of life. In the words of the BCP 1552: "Examine your lives and conversation by the rule of God's commandments, and whereinsoever ye shall perceive your selves to have offended, either by will, word, or deed, there bewail your own sinful lives, confess yourselves to almighty God with full purpose of amendment of life." This confession is, by nature, subjective in that the penitent has to be truly sorry for her sins yet the forgiveness and absolution a true penitent receives is not subjective at all, but wholly objective, assuming the penitent's "hearty repentance" and "true faith":

> Almighty God, our heavenly father, who of his great mercy, hath promised forgiveness of sins to all them, which with hearty repentance and true faith turn unto him: have mercy upon you, pardon and deliver you from all your sins, confirm and strength [*sic*] you in all goodness and bring you to everlasting life: through Jesus Christ our Lord. Amen.

Similarly, there is also the subjective nature of receiving the body and blood of Christ (*res et sacramentum*) by way of the bread and the wine (*sacramentum tantum*), and the objective nature of what the body and blood is doing to the worthy recipient (*res tantum*).[8] Subjectively the recipient is kneeling, receiving the bread in her hand, feeling its texture before tasting its flavor. She then receives

8. Historically, especially since the thirteenth century, theologians have understood that there is a threefold dimension to the sacraments: (1) *sacramentum tantum* = the sign only (e.g., bread and wine in the Eucharist or water and oil at baptism); (2) *res et sacramentum* = the reality and the sign (e.g., the bread and wine after consecration are both bread and wine *and* the body and blood of Jesus Christ); and (3) *res tantum* = the reality only (e.g., the union of members of the body of Christ to one another by way of our union with Jesus Christ). See King, "The Origin and Evolution of a Sacramental Formula."

the wine, feeling her lips on the chalice before tasting the wine. Her reactions to these moments and sensations of reception are subjective for she might be recalling to her mind Christ on the cross whereas the parishioner kneeling beside her might be offering a nonverbal prayer of thanksgiving. Both are experiencing the subjective nature of Communion. But what is happening objectively is exactly that—it is objectively happening. And this reality is that the reception of the body and blood of Christ, and the grace that comes thereby, unites the recipient to Christ: "Whoever feeds on my flesh and drinks my blood abides in me, and I in him" (John 6:56). And it also unites the recipient to others, bringing unity to the church of God: "we be very members incorporate in thy mystical body, which is the blessed company of all faithful people" (BCP 1552).

From these examples, then, we can see that the nature of the Christian faith is a combination of subjective and objective realities. One is not necessarily more important than the other. Rather, the two ideally come together in a subjective–objective balance, to use the language of Thornton. Thus, we must understand that throughout all areas of Anglican spirituality (and all Christian spirituality, in fact) there is the presence of the subjective and objective nature of the spiritual disciplines and practices. We should not reject the subjective nature in favor of a stiff and staid formalism nor should we think that a subjective and idiosyncratic enthusiasm is somehow more genuine, more "Spirit-ual." We need *both* for a proper balance and to exercise a true Anglican spirituality.

The immanent–transcendent balance

Second, the immanent–transcendent balance is a theological distinction made to indicate the two ends or "poles" of God's nature and his relationship to us, in that God is unknown yet known, hidden yet revealed.[9] By nature, God is transcendent: "The LORD is high above all nations, and his glory above the heavens! Who is

---

9. I am borrowing this language from Ware, *Orthodox Way*, 27. At its heart, the Eastern Orthodox discussion of the essence and energies of God is a discussion of God's transcendence and immanence, respectively.

like the LORD our God, who is seated on high, who looks far down on the heavens and the earth?" (Ps 113:4–6). Here the psalmist makes three observations of God's transcendence: he dwells in his rightful habitation, he has authority over all things in heaven and on earth, and he is not part of the creation but above it. This transcendence is also witnessed to in Acts 17:24 ("The God who made the world and everything in it, being Lord of heaven and earth, does not live in temples made by man") and Isa 40:22 ("It is he who sits above the circle of the earth"), for example. Transcendence refers to God's otherness, to the fact that he is wholly unlike his creation, including humans, and, therefore, beyond our understanding. It is less about God's "distance" from us and more about God being beyond our full comprehension.

But at the same time, God is also wholly immanent: "The LORD is near to all who call on him, to all who call on him in truth" (Ps 145:18); and, "Where shall I go from your Spirit? Or where shall I flee from your presence? If I ascend to heaven, you are there! If I make my bed in Sheol, you are there!" (Ps 139:7–8). Since the creation of the world God has, in some way, dwelt among and conversed with his creation: Adam and Eve "heard the sound of the LORD God walking in the garden in the cool of the day, and the man and his wife hid themselves from the presence of the LORD God among the trees of the garden" (Gen 3:8). God's presence was in the garden in such a way that Adam and Eve could hear the Lord walking. Though these references to God's presence and his walking are anthropomorphic, they are nonetheless conveying the truth that God is present with his people, for although he is wholly transcendent he is also wholly immanent.

Further, we need to look not only at God's immanence in a general fashion but also in its concrete manifestations; that is, by way of the incarnation of the Son of God and the sending of the Holy Spirit at Pentecost, for these ways of God's presence in the church are the necessary foundation stones for Christian spirituality, especially a spirituality, like Anglicanism, whose primary orientation is sacramental. In his *Why God Became Man*, Anselm of Canterbury (d. 1109) set out to explain why humankind's redemption could only be accomplished by God coming to earth as a human, dying and rising again. Anselm's guiding question is this: "By what logic or necessity did God become man, and by his death, as we believe and profess, restore life to the world, when he could have done this through the agency of some other person, angelic or human, or simply by willing it?"[10] Anselm then works out his theology of the incarnation of Jesus Christ, the God-Man, in such a way that it is intelligible to all, useful and logically beautiful. The point to note is this: God did not redeem fallen humankind in any way other than through the immanent activity of God, testified to most strikingly in Matthew's translation of the name Immanuel: "God with us" (Matt 1:23). Christian theology understands and teaches that Jesus Christ is the eternally begotten Son of God. He is "God from God, Light from Light, true God from true God, begotten, not made, of one Being with the Father; through him all things were made." It was "for us and for our salvation he came down from heaven, was incarnate from the Holy Spirit and the Virgin Mary, and was made man" (Nicene Creed). The transcendent God came to earth as a human for us. In the incomparable words of Charles Wesley (d. 1788),

> Christ, by highest Heav'n ador'd,
> Christ, the Everlasting Lord,
> Late in Time behold him come,
> Offspring of a Virgin's Womb.
> Veil'd in Flesh, the Godhead see,
> Hail th' Incarnate Deity!
> Pleas'd as Man with Men t' appear
> Jesus, our *Immanuel* here!

The implications of the incarnation for Christian spirituality are immense, for without the incarnation there would be no sacramental system, in particular there would be no Holy Eucharist with its corresponding sanctifying grace, removing an essential pillar from Anglican spirituality's tripartite rule of life. Prior to the incarnation of the Son of God, God's way of communing with his

---

10. Anselm of Canterbury, *Why God Became Man* 1.1; in *Anselm of Canterbury: The Major Works* (eds. Davies and Evans), 265.

people was through his "presence," though the manner of his presence was diverse and the "how" of his presence is often unclear in the Scriptures. For example, in Num 7:89 we learn that God's presence dwells and speaks from between the golden cherubim on the top of the ark of the covenant: "And when Moses went into the tent of meeting to speak with the LORD, he heard the voice speaking to him from above the mercy seat that was on the ark of the testimony, from between the two cherubim; and it spoke to him." At the same time God's presence was in the pillars of cloud and fire that led the Israelites through the wilderness (Exod 13:21, "And the LORD went before them by day in a pillar of cloud to lead them along the way, and by night in a pillar of fire to give them light") and he also alights on Mt. Sinai to talk with Moses (Exod 19:18, 20a, "Now Mount Sinai was wrapped in smoke because the LORD had descended on it in fire. . . . The LORD came down on Mount Sinai"). Was God present with his people prior to the incarnation of Jesus Christ? Yes. But with the incarnation the mode of God's presence is clear: he is a human person "who in every respect has been tempted as we are, yet without sin" (Heb 4:15). He "increased in wisdom and in stature and in favor with God and man" (Luke 2:52) and he felt emotions (John 11:35). He lived as a human among humans, he was fully human and fully God.

The incarnation then becomes the basis of the Christian sacramental system. Jesus told his followers in John 6:35, "I am the bread of life; whoever comes to me shall not hunger, and whoever believes in me shall never thirst." Just as God provided manna for the Israelites during their wilderness wanderings, which saved them from starvation and sustained them for the journey to the promised land, so too has God given his Son Jesus as the bread of life to his followers so that they will be saved and sated. But Jesus as the bread of life becomes concrete at the Last Supper when Jesus instructs his disciples that the blood and the wine of the supper become his body and blood, for the purpose, again, of saving and sustaining his followers. Though more will be said about the Holy Eucharist in chapter 3 below, what needs to be understood is that God is immanently present to us by way of his corporeal presence in the Holy Eucharist.

But God is also immanently present to his people by way of the indwelling Holy Spirit. Prior to the event of Pentecost, God the Holy Spirit did not permanently dwell within his people. He had an active ministry as the third person of the Holy Trinity (e.g., Gen 1:2; Judg 14:6, 19; 15:14) and whenever we are told prior to Pentecost that God dwelt with his people in his creation, we can assume that, in some way because of the unity of the persons of the Trinity, this includes the person of the Holy Spirit. But at Pentecost the manner by which the Holy Spirit is immanently present changed:

> When the day of Pentecost arrived, they were all together in one place. And suddenly there came from heaven a sound like a mighty rushing wind, and it filled the entire house where they were sitting. And divided tongues as of fire appeared to them and rested on each one of them. And they were all filled with the Holy Spirit and began to speak in other tongues as the Spirit gave them utterance. (Acts 2:1–4)

Jesus had promised the gift of the Holy Spirit to his followers (cf. John 14:16), as their divine Helper to carry out the work of making disciples of all the nations (Matt 28:19). Thus, the mission of the Holy Spirit is to assist God's people and God's church by indwelling us: "the Spirit of God dwells in you" (Rom 8:9). In these ways the utterly transcendent God is, at the same time, wholly immanent.

The individual–corporate balance

Third and lastly, let me say a bit more about the individual–corporate balance, one that is perhaps more important than ever. Again, in broad brushstrokes, the history of Christian spirituality began with individuals: Abram, Isaac, Jacob, the disciples and the apostle Paul, for example. That is, God is in the business of working with individual men and women, but these individuals are always a part of the people of God (whether Israel or the church). In Gen 12:2 God promises that Abram will be the father of a "great nation." This promise, returned to again and again throughout the Scriptures (e.g., Gen 15:1–5; Gal 3:15–18), is explained this way by Isaac to his son Jacob: "God Almighty bless you and make you fruitful and multiply you, that you may become a company of peoples" (Gen 28:3). This language of a "company of peoples" or "great nation" demonstrates that though God works in and with individual persons, there is no individualism in the economy of God. In the words of Vatican II's Dogmatic Constitution on the Church, *Lumen gentium*:

> At all times and in every race God has given welcome to whosoever fears Him and does what is right. God, however, does not make men holy and save them merely as individuals, without bond or link between one another. Rather has it pleased Him to bring men together as one people, a people which acknowledges Him in truth and serves Him in holiness.[11]

God works with individuals but individuals who are necessarily part of a bigger whole—the people of God. Simply put, the church is *not* a voluntary society of people who choose to be in the church. Being an adopted son or daughter of God by definition means that you *are* the church. Hence the theological truth that "there is no salvation outside the Church," to use the words of Cyprian of Carthage (d. 258).[12] There is no way to be saved apart from the church, the body of Christ. To err toward the individualistic is to risk thinking of one's faith and one's spirituality as a "me and Jesus" affair. To err on the other side is to negate the individual's need to have a personal faith, resulting in an unorthodox universalism. A proper individual–corporate balance sees the importance of both the person in relationship to God and the fact that God ordained his divine institutions to be a means of grace to his people, for it is through the church that the graces won by Christ are given to his followers. In the words of *Lumen gentium* again:

> Basing itself upon Sacred Scripture and Tradition, it [i.e., the council] teaches that the Church, now sojourning on earth as an exile, is necessary for salvation. Christ,

11. Vatican II, *Lumen Gentium* 9.

12. Cyprian, *Ep.* 73.21.2, in Cyprian, *Letters of St. Cyprian of Carthage* (trans. Clarke), 66.

present to us in His Body, which is the Church, is the one Mediator and the unique way of salvation. In explicit terms He Himself affirmed the necessity of faith and baptism and thereby affirmed also the necessity of the Church, for through baptism as through a door men enter the Church. Whosoever, therefore, knowing that the Catholic Church was made necessary by Christ, would refuse to enter or to remain in it, could not be saved.[13]

And a proper balance between the individual and the corporate is absolutely essential in Anglican spirituality for we are part of the Catholic tradition but we also believe in personal conviction and conversion. Thus, a true Anglican spirituality will hold all three of these variables in tension, seeing in each of them an important element of genuine Christian existence.

13. Vatican II, *Lumen gentium* 14.

2

The Daily Office

Set Times for Prayer

THE ORIGIN OF THE Christian practice of praying at set times of the day goes back to Jewish history and practice.[1] In the earliest history of the church we read that the first Christians attended the temple together each day for "the prayers" (Acts 2:42–46). The practices of prayer in Second Temple Judaism varied but that there were patterns of fixed daily prayer is not debated.[2] The first Christians, then, mostly of Jewish background, were already acclimated to daily prayer, so it is not surprising that early Christians would adopt the practice. By the time of the *On the Apostolic Tradition*, dated to the third century, fixed daily prayer was so common that the author(s) of the text include a chapter "On the time when it is proper to pray," arguing for prayer in the morning; at the third, sixth and ninth hours; "before your body rests on the

1. Ps 55:17, for example: "Evening and morning and at noon I utter my complaint and moan, and he hears my voice."

2. Penner, *Patterns of Daily Prayer*.

14

bed"; and "around midnight." And these fixed times of prayer were not just for monks but for "every faithful man and woman."[3] In other words, fixed daily prayer was a practice of the church, not the monastery. It was expected of all faithful people, not just those living the monastic life. Nonetheless, the role of monastics in the history of the church, and in influencing prayer practices, cannot be underestimated.

Monastic Foundations

Benedictine monks played a major role in early and medieval English Christian history.[4] It began when Gregory the Great (d. 604) sent Benedictine monks to England in 598 to "evangelize" the island.[5] Born in or around 540 to a prominent yet pious family, Gregory spent his early career in public service but in the mid-570s he became a monk, founding a monastery (dedicated to St. Andrew the apostle) on his family's property on the Caelian Hill in Rome.[6] In Gregory's estimation, he entered "the safe harbor of the monastery, having left behind all that belongs to the world."[7] Soon thereafter Gregory was made one of the seven deacons of Rome[8] and appointed ambassador to Constantinople (from 579/80 to 585/86) by Pope Pelagius II (d. 590). Around 585 Gregory returned to Rome and monastic life at St. Andrew's and was chosen pope after the death of Pelagius II (February 8, 590), being consecrated on September 3, 590. It is well known that before he was elected pope, Gregory heard about slaves in Rome who were "fair-skinned and light-haired" Angles.[9] Seeing an opportunity to enlarge the

3. Hippolytus, *On the Apostolic Tradition* (trans. Stewart-Sykes), 164–65.

4. Knowles, *Monastic Order.*

5. Cristina Ricci, "Gregory's Missions to the Barbarians," in Neil and Del Santo, eds., *Companion to Gregory,* 47–55.

6. In total Gregory founded seven monasteries, six in Sicily and one in Rome. See Gregory of Tours, *History of the Franks* 10.1.

7. *Letter to Leander* 1, in Gregory the Great, *Moral Reflections* (trans. Kerns), 47.

8. Symonds, "Deacons," 408–9.

9. Anonymous, *Earliest Life* (trans. Colgrave), 91.

kingdom of God, Gregory emancipated and sent these men back to England to spread the faith. Two letters penned by Gregory tell us that these men became monks at Gregory's monastery on the Caelian Hill prior to their mission to the Anglo-Saxons: "we have decided for this reason that Augustine, a monk . . . should be sent there with other monks"; and, "we have taken care to send there . . . Augustine, a monk . . . together with other monks, so that through them we might learn the wishes of the people themselves and consider their conversion."[10]

From this monastic seed grew a sizeable and extensive tree of monasteries that became an essential fabric of the English church and English spirituality. Around the year 1500, there were approximately nine hundred monasteries in England, housing nearly twelve thousand monks, nuns, canons, and friars.[11] These men and women were voluntarily joining communities in their late teens and early twenties and many were from the middle or lower ranks of society.[12] In other words, the monastic life was an attractive option for those looking for a life of service to God. Further, Benedictine monasticism's contribution to the establishment of many important cathedrals and schools in England is unique in European history. According to monastic historian James Clark, "By the turn of the fifteenth century, the Black Monks [i.e., the Benedictines] undoubtedly formed the largest community, religious or secular, at either university [that is, at Oxford or Cambridge]."[13] Bede Thomas Mudge writes,

> The influence of the Benedictine tradition was part of the air that every medieval English person breathed. From one's earliest years, through education and into whatever station in life a person belonged, the influence of the Abbey or Priory was never far away. . . . The monastic offices and masses were commonly attended

10. Gregory the Great, *Letters* (trans. Martyn), 438 and 444.

11. Clark, "The Religious Orders in Pre-Reformation England," in Clark, ed., *Religious*, 7.

12. Bernard, *Late Medieval English Church*, 166–67.

13. Clark, "Religious Orders," 20.

by the public; monastic spirituality was respected; and abbot and monk were part of the common scene. . . . [T]he example and influence of the Benedictine monastery, with its rhythm of divine office and eucharist, the tradition of learning and the *lectio divina*, and the family relationship among abbot and community were determinative for much English life.[14]

Further, there are many liturgical similarities between medieval English monasticism and Anglicanism. Though it was most usual in the Middle Ages for monastics to pray seven (or even eight) times a day in community, the central services of worship going all the way back to the patristic era were Morning and Evening Prayer.[15] These times of prayer, along with the Eucharist, became the central acts of worship in the Anglican tradition: "monastic theology and liturgical expression were inscribed and thus preserved in the BCP and in the influential writings of the Caroline divines."[16]

[The] BCP continued the basic monastic pattern of the Eucharist and the divine office, in the form of "mattins" (which basically combined the offices of vigils and lauds) and "evensong" (drawing from the offices of vespers and compline) as the principal public forms of worship.[17] . . . Daily celebration of mattins and evensong in the nonparochial churches [such as cathedrals] . . . is fully documented from the late seventeenth century onwards. Yet statistics indicate that the daily celebration of the hours in many parishes continued as well, even though there seems to have been an eighteenth-century slump in religious practice in England in general, followed by a significant nineteenth-century restoration owing, at least in part, to the Oxford Movement.[18]

---

14. Mudge, "Monastic Spirituality," 507.

15. See Guiver, *Company of Voices*, 52–53.

16. Pauley, "Implication," 263.

17. See Ketley, ed., *The Two Liturgies*, 19.

18. Pauley, "Implication," 265.

This monastic quality to early Anglican liturgy seems to owe much to Thomas Cranmer's love of the Bible and of the patristic readings of Scripture that led him into a more monastic understanding of the liturgical hours: "Just as the 'monastic' understanding of liturgical prayer in early monasticism emphasized listening to and being formed by the words of Scripture, rather than singing and speaking them primarily in an attitude of praise, so too did Cranmer believe that the Bible was the living Word of God. . . . [H]is ideal was that the liturgy should play its significant role in encouraging everyone to 'heare, read, marke, learne, and inwardly digeste'"[19] the Scriptures, to which we shall return momentarily.

> The seventeenth century was also an era of order in religious practice. This meant not only the order of the liturgical hours but also the order of other aspects of daily life in connection with prayer. Prayers were composed for everyday occasions: on walking, dressing, grace before meals, on starting a journey. This practice of prayers for the daily activities of life finds a counterpart in the RB [Rule of Benedict]. As the RB strives to cultivate an habitual sense of the presence of God in alternating periods of prayer and work, so does the BCP.[20]

In the astute words of Martin Thornton:

> It is again necessary to look at the historical setting, for the Book of Common Prayer is derived from a long line of ancestors, ultimately from the Benedictine *Regula*, with which, ascetically, it has much in common: both are designed to regulate the total life of a community, centered on the Divine Office, the Mass, and continuous devotion as daily, domestic life unfolds. Both are concerned with common, even "family" prayer. Neither are missals, breviaries or lay manuals, because here the priest–lay division does not apply: they are common prayer, prayer for the united Church or community.[21]

19. Pauley, "Implication," 266, quoting from the Collect for the Second Sunday of Advent.

20. Pauley, "Implication," 268.

21. Martin Thornton, "The Anglican Spiritual Tradition," in Holloway, ed., *Anglican Tradition*, 74.

In short, the Daily Office, so essential to Anglicanism and Anglican spirituality, is of monastic origin and that makes a difference as to how we should understand the spirituality of the Daily Office.

According to the Preface to the BCP 1549, written by Cranmer,

> There was never any thing by the wit of man so well devised, or so surely established, which (in continuance of time) hath not been corrupted: as (among other things) it may plainly appear by the common prayers in the Church, commonly called divine service: the first original and ground whereof, if a man would search out by the ancient fathers, he shall find that the same was not ordained, but of a good purpose, and for a great advancement of godliness: For they so ordered the matter, that all the whole Bible (or the greatest part thereof) should be read over once in the year, intending thereby, that the Clergy, and specially such as were Ministers of the congregation, should (by often reading and meditation of God's word) be stirred up to godliness themselves, and be more able also to exhort other by wholesome doctrine, and to confute them that were adversaries to the truth. And further, that the people (by daily hearing of holy scripture read in the Church) should continually profit more and more in the knowledge of God, and be the more inflamed with the love of his true religion.

He goes on to say, "the very pure word of God, the holy scriptures, or that which is evidently grounded upon the same; and that in such a language and order, as is most easy and plain for the understanding, both of the readers and hearers." Notice that the whole Bible (or nearly all of it) was to be read every year in order to stir up its readers to holiness. Moreover, "the people (by daily hearing of holy scripture read in the Church) should continually profit more and more in the knowledge of God, and be the more inflamed with the love of his true religion." The whole purpose of Anglican worship is "for a great advancement of godliness."

The Word of God

The particular spirituality of the Daily Office is summed up well in its emphasis on formation and transformation by and under the Word of God.[22] Perhaps one of the most well-known Collects in the BCP is for the Second Sunday of Advent: "Blessed Lord, who hast caused all holy Scriptures to be written for our learning; Grant that we may in such wise hear them, read, mark, learn, and inwardly digest them, that by patience and comfort of thy holy Word, we may embrace, and ever hold fast, the blessed hope of everlasting life, which thou hast given us in our Saviour Jesus Christ. Amen" (BCP 1928). The Daily Office lectionary exposes the one who prays to almost the whole of the biblical text. It immerses the Daily Office practitioner in salvation history, recounting the story of God's creation, humanity's fall, and our redemption, while also marking that same salvation history through the seasons of the liturgical year. In the words of the late liturgical scholar Robert Taft, the Daily Office takes its "meaning from that which alone gives meaning to all of these things: the paschal mystery of salvation in Christ Jesus."[23] Thus, it is the story of God and the story of humankind and should be, then, heard, read, marked, and learned. But just as importantly, according to the collect, the Word of God must be inwardly digested.

This collect, composed by Cranmer for the BCP 1549, is based on Romans 15:4 ("For whatsoever things were written aforetime were written for our learning, that we through patience and comfort of the scriptures might have hope" [KJV]), which is the first verse of the Epistle reading for the day in the BCPs 1549 and 1928. The use of the word "learning" in the Collect does not mean memorization but "instruction." Thus, we *hear* God's Word, *read* it, *mark* it, and are *instructed by* it, leading to patience and comfort. This "instruction" by the Word is intimately connected to the work of Christ, our Teacher.

22. See Null, "Thomas Cranmer."
23. Taft, *Liturgy of the Hours*, 334; see also 334–38.

In 389 Augustine of Hippo (d. 430) wrote a work entitled *On the Teacher*, which was cast in the form of a discussion between him and his sixteen-year-old son Adeodatus. After many chapters on the nature of words as signs ("a thing which of itself makes some other thing come to mind"),[24] Augustine says that even when signs are presented to us, including words, we are "ignorant of the reality of which it is a sign."[25] A sign needs to be connected to the thing signified. When we want to teach a baby the meaning of the word "mama," we say "mama" and point to her mother. When we teach the color "black" we point to something that is black. Thus, to learn, to be instructed, we need someone to connect the sign to the thing signified. In and of themselves, says Augustine, words simply suggest that there is a reality that we need to look for that is signified by that word. He writes:

> Words . . . serve merely to suggest we look for realities. . . . By means of words, therefore, we learn nothing but words; in fact, only the sound and noise of words. For if things which are not signs cannot be words, then, even though I have already heard a word, I do not know it is a word until I know what it signifies. Consequently, with the knowledge of realities there also comes the knowledge of the words.[26]

The one who connects the signs and the things signified "is not a speaker who utters sounds exteriorly . . . but . . . [He who] presides within, over the mind itself. . . . And He who is consulted, . . . He it is who teaches . . . [, and He is] Christ."[27]

To prove his point, Augustine quotes from the apostle Paul's letter to the Ephesians: "that Christ may dwell in your hearts through faith" (3:17). Though the apostle is thinking about the supernatural presence of Christ through grace, Augustine applies these words to the natural order in as much as God is present

---

24. Augustine, *On Christian Teaching* 2.1.1 (trans. Green, 30).

25. Augustine, *The Teacher* 10.33 (trans. Colleran, 173).

26. Augustine, *The Teacher* 10.36 (trans. Colleran, 175–76).

27. Augustine, *The Teacher* 10.38 (trans. Colleran, 177).

in each human; therefore, Christ is within each person.[28] This is possible because he is the Eternal Word (John 1:1–2) and as the Λόγος he is of the mind or reason of humankind (*logos* = logical). Our rationality and reasoning ability are because Christ is within us. In the words of John 1:9: the Word was the "true light, which gives light to everyone." Blaise Pascal (d. 1662) also posits an inner teacher, or inner epistemological faculty, when he writes, "We know the truth not only through our reason but also through our heart. It is through the latter that we know first principles, and reason, which has nothing to do with it, tries in vain to refute them."[29] The Christian tradition is rich with the notion that God is our true inner Teacher.

Thus, we are instructed by the Word of God during the Daily Office because Christ the Teacher is instructing us from within. Of course, just as we can suppress the truth that comes from without, we can just as easily suppress the truth from within: "Do not quench the Spirit" (1 Thess 5:19). Aids to our instruction by Christ the Teacher come in the forms of grace and the illumination of the Holy Spirit, both gained at baptism. That grace is given at baptism is bound up with its very nature as a sacrament, so nothing more needs to be said.

The two main scriptural texts that speak to illumination, however, are: "For it is impossible, in the case of those who have once been enlightened, who have tasted the heavenly gift, and have shared in the Holy Spirit" (Heb 6:4); and "But recall the former days when, after you were enlightened, you endured a hard struggle with sufferings" (Heb 10:32). The former passage ties baptismal enlightenment to the work of the Holy Spirit who "will guide you into all truth" (John 16:13), though "the gift of the Spirit is distinct from the baptismal enlightenment."[30] What the author of Hebrews means when he refers to a tasting of the "heavenly gift" is an impartation of divine knowledge. According to the New

28. See Colleran's endnote on Augustine, *The Teacher* 11.38 (trans. Colleran, 235).

29. Pascal, *Pensées* 110 (trans. Krailsheimer, 28).

30. Ysebaert, *Greek Baptismal Terminology*, 172.

Testament, when we are baptized we are illumined, given a gift of divine knowledge that then works with the inner Christ, the Teacher, to help us be instructed by the biblical text during our praying of the Daily Office.

It was Justin Martyr (d. ca. 167) who first referred to the illuminative nature of baptism: "this washing is called illumination, as those who learn these things are illuminated in the mind."[31] Clement of Alexandria (d. ca. 215) makes the connection between baptism and illumination explicit: "when we were reborn . . . we were enlightened, that is, we came to the knowledge of God." Likewise, "when we are baptized, we are enlightened."[32] Again, the gift of the Holy Spirit is distinct in these authors from baptismal illumination. Justin Martyr in particular reminds us that in addition to baptismal illumination, the Christian is also given the sevenfold gift of the Holy Spirit, which we now link with Confirmation in particular.[33] This sevenfold gift of the Spirit comes from the Vulgate rendering of Isa 11:2–3: "And the spirit of the Lord shall rest upon him: the spirit of wisdom, and of understanding, the spirit of counsel, and of fortitude, the spirit of knowledge, and of godliness. And he shall be filled with the spirit of the fear of the Lord" (Douay-Rheims). We see there gifts of wisdom, understanding, and knowledge, all of which aid the Daily Office pray-er in being instructed.

But let us return now to the last element of the Collect for the Second Sunday of Advent: inwardly digesting God's word. As I said, this Collect was written by Cranmer, so the language of "inwardly digest" is original with him and seems to have no direct precedent in patristic or medieval literature or liturgical documents. The language of "digest," however, suggests a monastic origin of the term, which is not surprising given the prayer book's monastic genesis. Digestion suggests eating, and eating suggests chewing. In the high Middle Ages, the process of divine reading had been codified into four stages or stairs on a ladder. In the *Ladder of Monks* (*Scala*

---

31. Justin Martyr, *First Apology* 61(trans. Barnard, 67).

32. Clement of Alexandria, *Christ the Educator* 1.25.1 and 1.26.1 (trans. Wood, 24–26).

33. Justin Martyr, *Dialogue with Trypho* 39.2.

Claustralium), the twelfth-century Carthusian monk Guigo II (d. 1188) wrote that there are four rungs on a ladder that enable us to reach contemplation: (1) reading; (2) meditation; (3) prayer; and (4) contemplation. It is the second rung, meditation, that I think Cranmer has in mind when he talks about inwardly digesting the Holy Scriptures. Meditation is a gift that is given from above and is the result of both baptismal illumination and the gifts of the Holy Spirit. The primary activity of meditation is *ruminatio*, which is "an image of regurgitation,"[34] of digesting food. Gregory the Great, in his *Pastoral Care*, wrote that the

> mind is commonly signified by the term "belly" because, as the belly consumes food, so the mind assimilates the cares by brooding over them. We are taught that the mind is called the belly by that sentence in which it is written: *The spirit of a man is the lamp of the Lord, which searcheth all the hidden things of the bowels* [Prov 20:27]. This as if it had been said that the illumination of divine inspiration, entering the mind of man, shows the mind to itself by enlightening it.[35]

Here we see several themes come together: baptismal illumination, meditation as eating with the resulting enlightenment of knowledge. Similarly, Hugh of St. Victor (d. 1141) says that we need "to recall [the principles we have gleaned from our readings] from the stomach of memory to taste them."[36] In other words, to "inwardly digest" is to ruminate, to chew the cud, if you will, of the Scriptures so that we are nourished by the words and our minds are fed and nourished with the truth of God's Word. In the words of the homily "A Fruitful Exhortation to the Reading of Scripture":

34. Carruthers, *Book of Memory*, 206.

35. Gregory the Great, *Pastoral Care* 3.12 (trans. Davis, 124–25). Compare with the Benedictine-turned-Cistercian William of St. Thierry (d. 1148): "Some part of your daily [scriptural] reading should also each day be committed to memory, taken in as it were into the stomach, to be more carefully digested and brought up again for frequent rumination." William of St. Thierry, *The Golden Epistle* 123 (trans. Berkeley, 52).

36. Hugh of St. Victor, *Didascalion* 3.11, in Harkins and van Liere, eds., *Interpretation of Scripture*, 126–27.

And there is nothing that so much strengtheneth our faith and trust in God, that so much keepeth up innocency and pureness of the heart, and also of outward godly life and conversation, as continual reading and recording of God's word. For that thing, which by continual use of reading of Holy Scripture, and diligent searching of the same, is deeply printed and graven in the heart, at length turneth almost into nature.[37]

Hence the repetitive nature of the Daily Office is a good thing! For it allows us to come back again and again, year after year, to the same readings so that we can regurgitate them and chew on them again. And the *telos* of this hearing, reading, marking, learning, and inwardly digesting is not some sort of domesticated, Enlightenment-esque knowledge, for God's word excels all sciences.[38] Rather, the *telos* is the spiritual gift of wisdom. And what is wisdom: "she is a breath of the power of God, and a pure emanation of the glory of the Almighty, . . . she is the reflection of eternal light, a spotless mirror of the working of God, and an image of his goodness" (Wis 7:25–26 RSV). It is not scriptural mastery but formation in Christlikeness, for the "hearing and keeping of [Scripture] maketh us blessed."[39] The literal reading of the Scriptures never stops there but always moves on to what medieval theologians called the *tropological*, which "is what the text means to us when we turn its words, like a mirror, upon ourselves, how we understand it when we have domesticated it and made it our own, and that is the special activity of . . . *meditatio*."[40] For "these books [of the Scriptures] therefore ought to be much in our hands, in our eyes, in our ears, in our mouths, but most of all in our hearts."[41]

---

37. Bray, ed., *Books of Homilies*, 9.

38. Bray, ed., *Books of Homilies*, 10.

39. Bray, ed., *Books of Homilies*, 8.

40. Carruthers, *Book of Memory*, 210.

41. Bray, ed., *Books of Homilies*, 8.

The Spirituality of the Daily Office

For the apostle Paul, "liturgy *is* Christian life."[42] Think of Rom 12:1: "I appeal to you therefore, brothers, by the mercies of God, to present your bodies as a living sacrifice, holy and acceptable to God, which is your spiritual worship"; or, Heb 13:15: "let us continually offer up a sacrifice of praise to God, that is, the fruit of lips that acknowledge his name." What we do in liturgy, especially in the Daily Office, is "exactly what the New Testament itself did with Christ, . . . it applied him and what he was and is to the present."[43] The New Testament and the Daily Office tells us again and again the holy history of Jesus as a perpetual *anamnesis* (remembering):

> That which was from the beginning, which we have heard, which we have seen with our eyes, which we looked upon and have touched with our hands, concerning the word of life—the life was made manifest, and we have seen it, and testify to it and proclaim to you the eternal life, which was with the Father and was made manifest to us—that which we have seen and heard we proclaim also to you, so that you too may have fellowship with us; and indeed our fellowship is with the Father and with his Son Jesus Christ. And we are writing these things so that our joy may be complete. (1 John 1:1–4)

Simply put, the end of the Daily Office is not just our formation under the Word of God, but our glory in Christ and our "conversion into Christ."[44] "Every liturgical celebration of the Church," writes Mark Searle, including the Daily Office, "is an attempt to facilitate the experience of conversion by ritualizing it."[45] The Daily Office, then, is a celebration of the Christian life, of our ongoing union with God in Christ. Cyprian of Carthage (d. 258) says that we pray in the morning to celebrate the resurrection of our Lord, that act which effected our salvation. "Likewise at sunset and the

---

42. Taft, *Liturgy of the Hours*, 336.
43. Taft, *Liturgy of the Hours*, 336.
44. Taft, *Liturgy of the Hours*, 345.
45. Searle, "Journey of Conversion," 49.

decline of day must we needs pray again," he writes. "For since Christ is the true Sun and the true Day, when we pray at the decline of the world's sun and day and entreat that the light may again come upon us, we are asking for the [Second] Advent of Christ, which will bestow on us the grace of eternal life."[46] Thus, when we pray in the evening and/or at night we are asking for our full and final salvation where we will be united with Christ in the eternal Jerusalem, where there will only be day and light.

The spirituality, if you will, of Morning Prayer is expressed beautifully by a handful of authors, a few of whom will serve as illustrations. First, Dietrich Bonhoeffer (d. 1945) wrote that in the Old Testament the day began at evening and ended at sundown, which for him was a time of expectation. Whereas in the New Testament, the day begins, like our day, at the break of day and ends with dawn the next day, which for Bonhoeffer is a time of fulfillment, especially when seen thorough the resurrection of the Lord.[47] In the early Christian tradition, Morning Prayer was a time "to consecrate the day to the works of God, to thank him for his benefits received, especially the benefit of redemption in the rising of his Son, to rekindle our desire for him as a remedy against sin during the beginning day, and to ask for continued help."[48] As John Cassian (d. 435) writes,

> When they wake up out of sleep and arise with something like a renewed joy after their slumber and, before conceiving any thought in their heart or letting in a memory or care concerning business, they consecrate the source and beginning of their thoughts by divine holocausts, what are they doing in fact but presenting their firstfruits through the high priest Jesus Christ, for use in this life and in the form of a daily resurrection?[49]

Lastly, a word about the spirituality of Evening Prayer. The passing of the day and impending darkness reminds us of the

---

46. Cyprian, *On the Lord's Prayer* 35 (trans. Bindley, 68).

47. Bonhoeffer, *Life Together*, 40.

48. Taft, *Liturgy of the Hours*, 354.

49. John Cassian, *Conferences* 21.26.1 (trans. Ramsey, 739).

darkness of Christ's passion and death and of the passing nature of all creation in anticipation of the glorious and eternal light of the new heavens and new earth. Basil the Great (d. 379) writes, "When the day is finished, thanksgiving should be offered for what has been given us during the day or for what we have done rightly, and confession made for what we have failed to do . . . propitiating God in our prayers for all our failings."[50]

50. Basil of Caesarea, *Longer Rules* 37.4, cited in Taft, *Liturgy of the Hours*, 355.

3

The Holy Eucharist

PERHAPS NOTHING IS MORE contentious among Anglicans than to talk about the theology of the Holy Eucharist. In this chapter I would like to get at the heart of Anglican common life—partaking of the body and blood of Jesus Christ. Recall that the Anglican *regula* is the Daily Office, Holy Eucharist, and private devotion. Though it was not originally meant to be so, the Daily Office is often said alone. Again, that is not always the case but I would imagine that it is often the case. That being so, we start with the theological truth that there is no solitary or individual Holy Eucharist, for the very celebration of the Sacred Mystery is an act of bringing unity and proclaiming unity.

The Centrality of the Sacrament of the Holy Eucharist

Even though the apostle Paul begins 1 Corinthians 11 by pointing out errors in the Corinthian church, notice that even there his language is about *the community*, the body of Christ: "when you come together" (vv. 17–18 and 20). The very act of coming together for the Lord's Supper is an act of *communion* (from *communis* =

29

common). And explicitly in the same book: "The cup of blessing that we bless, is it not a participation in the blood of Christ? The bread that we break, is it not a participation in the body of Christ? Because there is one bread, we who are many are one body, for we all partake of the one bread" (10:16–17). "The Church," as the body of Christ, "draws her life from the Eucharist."[1] Our unity is confected by the Eucharist and our unity is confessed in the Eucharist. Thus, the Holy Eucharist is the center of the life of the church and it is that to which the Daily Office prepares and from which personal devotion flows. To quote the Second Vatican Council, the Eucharist is "the source and summit of the Christian life."[2]

The Holy Eucharist is the source of our Christian life, primarily because as a sacrament it conveys grace. The Collect for Maundy Thursday says:

> Almighty Father, whose dear Son, on the night before he suffered, did institute the Sacrament of his Body and Blood; Mercifully grant that we may thankfully receive the same in remembrance of him, who in these holy mysteries giveth us a pledge of life eternal; the same thy Son Jesus Christ our Lord, who now liveth and reigneth with thee and the Holy Spirit ever, one God, world without end. *Amen.* (BCP 1928)[3]

Christ instituted the Eucharist as a sacrament and according to the 39 Articles of Religion, a sacrament is "ordained of Christ . . . as not only badges or tokens of Christian men's profession, but rather they be certain sure witnesses, and effectual signs of grace, and God's

1. John Paul II, *Ecclesia de Eucharistia* 1.

2. Vatican II, *Lumen gentium* 11; and *Catechism of the Catholic Church* 1324.

3. Though the origins of this Collect only go back the BCP 1928 Revision Committee, it is remarkably close to a Collect written by Thomas Aquinas for the Feast of Corpus Christi: "O Lord Jesus Christ, who in a wonderful sacrament hast left unto us a memorial of thy passion: Grant us, we beseech thee, so to venerate the Sacred Mysteries of thy Body and Blood, that we may ever perceive within ourselves the fruit of thy redemption; who livest and reignest with the Father in the unity of the Holy Spirit, God, for ever and ever." Shepherd, *Oxford American Prayer Book*, 153.

good will towards us, by the which he doth work invisibly in us, and doth not only quicken, but also strengthen and confirm our Faith in him" (Article 25). Notice that the Eucharist is a sure witness and effectual sign of grace. As an "effectual sign" it rightly and accurately points to the greater reality, which in the Holy Eucharist is the literal body and blood of Jesus Christ: "This *is* my body.... This cup *is* ... my blood." As witness it testifies to the presence of grace in God's economy of salvation and grace is the very thing (*res*) that we need to be in relationship to God; it is "the inward working of God's free mercy" that seals "in our hearts the promises of God."[4] It also effects "our holiness and joining in Christ."[5]

The Eucharist is a sure witness and effectual sign of "God's good will towards us." Notice the note of intimacy to the Holy Eucharist—it is God's good will toward me, toward you. God's good will is evidenced to us by his desire that we be saved, for God "is patient toward [us], not wishing that any should perish, but that all should reach repentance" (2 Pet 3:9). In the words of the great spiritual theologian Thomas à Kempis (d. 1471): "I have given my very Body and Blood to be your food, that I may be all yours, and that you may be mine for ever."[6] God wants us to be sanctified, made holy, for "this is the will of God, [our] sanctification" (1 Thess 4:3). Thomas Cranmer says it this way: "Christ ordained the sacrament to move and stir all men to friendship, love, and concord, and to put away all hatred, variance, and discord, and to testify to brotherly and unfeigned love between all them that be the members of Christ.... And that finally by his means they may enjoy with him the glory and kingdom of heaven."[7]

---

4. *Second Book of Homilies*, "An Homily Wherein is Declared that Common Prayer and Sacraments Ought to be Ministered in a Tongue that is Understanded to the Hearers," in Bray, ed., *Books of Homilies*, 355.

5. *Second Book of Homilies*, "An Homily Wherein is Declared that Common Prayer and Sacraments Ought to be Ministered in a Tongue that is Understanded to the Hearers," in Bray, ed., *Books of Homilies*, 357.

6. Thomas à Kempis, *Imitation of Christ* 4.8 (trans. Sherley-Price, 198).

7. Thomas Cranmer, *Defensio verae et catholicae doctrinae de sacramento* 1.7, in Cranmer, *Archbishop Cranmer*, 10–11.

Further, the Eucharist works invisibly by quickening, strengthening, and confirming our faith. Regarding our quickening, the apostle Paul says to the Corinthians, "'The first man Adam became a living being'; the last Adam became a life-giving spirit" (1 Cor 15:45). The context here is resurrection and life. Thus, when we are quickened we are given resurrection life; that is, we are made like Jesus Christ, for our faith is made alive. Regarding our strengthening, we "can do all things through him who strengthens" us (Phil 4:13). We are strengthened in order to do the work that we have been given to do, for our living faith orients the direction of our lives of service: "we humbly beseech thee, O heavenly Father, so to assist us with thy grace, that we may continue in that holy fellowship, and do all such good works as thou hast prepared for us to walk in" (BCP 1928).[8] Lastly, regarding confirming, I again quote the apostle Paul to the church in Corinth: "Grace to you and peace from God our Father and the Lord Jesus Christ. I give thanks to my God always for you because of the grace of God that was given you in Christ Jesus, that in every way you were enriched in him in all speech and all knowledge—even as the testimony about Christ was confirmed among you—so that you are not lacking in any gift, as you wait for the revealing of our Lord Jesus Christ, who will sustain you to the end, guiltless in the day of our Lord Jesus Christ" (1 Cor 1:3–8). Though our faith may oftentimes be shaky, God's will for us is that our faith be firm and unwavering and it is the Eucharist and its operative grace that effects the confirmation of our faith. The whole reason that Christ instituted the Holy Eucharist, writes Cranmer, is to "confirm [our] faith and hope of eternal salvation."[9]

The Theology of the Prayer of Humble Access

We see all of this rich theology contained in the "Prayer of Humble Access," which dates back to the Order of Communion from 1548,

8. See chapter 5 for a further discussion of this Post-Communion Prayer.

9. Cranmer, *Defensio verae et catholicae doctrinae de sacramento* 1.Pref, in Cranmer, *Archbishop Cranmer*, xxii.

predating even the first BCP, which was published in 1549. In the BCP 1928 rendering:

> We do not presume to come to this thy Table, O merciful Lord, trusting in our own righteousness, but in thy manifold and great mercies. We are not worthy so much as to gather up the crumbs under thy Table. But thou art the same Lord, whose property is always to have mercy: Grant us therefore, gracious Lord, so to eat the flesh of thy dear Son Jesus Christ, and to drink his blood, that our sinful bodies may be made clean by his Body, and our souls washed through his most precious Blood, and that we may evermore dwell in him, and he in us. Amen.

The earlier elements of the prayer contain allusions to Mark 7:27–28 where Jesus says, "It is not meet to take the children's bread, and to cast it unto the dogs," and the gentile woman replies, "Yes, Lord: yet the dogs under the table eat of the children's crumbs" (KJV). It also refers to Luke 7:6, where a centurion says to Jesus, "Lord, trouble not thyself: for I am not worthy that thou shouldest enter under my roof" (KJV). Though the latter section of the prayer has no direct biblical citations, which are so common in other parts of the Communion liturgy, there are, of course, the common biblical themes of being washed and made clean. For example, Ps 51:7 says, "Purge me with hyssop, and I shall be clean: wash me, and I shall be whiter than snow." Or, 1 Cor 6:11 where the apostle Paul reminds the Corinthian believers that they "were washed, . . . were sanctified, . . . were justified in the name of the Lord Jesus Christ and by the Spirit of our God."

The language of "so to eat the flesh of thy dear Son Jesus Christ, and to drink his blood" clearly derives from Jesus' Bread of Life discourse in John 6:47–58, which says in part: "So Jesus said to them, 'Truly, truly, I say to you, unless you eat the flesh of the Son of Man and drink his blood, you have no life in you. Whoever feeds on my flesh and drinks my blood has eternal life, and I will raise him up on the last day. For my flesh is true food, and my blood is true drink. Whoever feeds on my flesh and drinks my blood abides in me, and I in him'" (vv. 53–56).

Regarding the phrase "that our sinful bodies may be made clean by his Body, and our souls washed through his most precious Blood," Thomas Cranmer borrowed it from earlier medieval Missals that said, "As we have committed sins of flesh and blood, may the flesh of our Lord Jesus Christ make us clean and his blood wash us."[10] There also seems to be a reliance on Heb 10:22: "Let us draw near with a true heart in full assurance of faith, having our hearts sprinkled from an evil conscience and our bodies washed with pure water"; or even Lev 17:11: "For the life of the flesh is in the blood: and I have given it to you upon the altar to make an atonement for your souls: for it is the blood that maketh an atonement for the soul" (KJV).

Concerning its location in the liturgy and what theological implications this may signal, it is a prayer of humble thankfulness for worthy reception rather than a prayer of repentance. After all, the prayer comes *after* the declaration of Absolution and the assurance of the Comfortable Words, if they are used. As one scholar notes, "In the Protestant perspective of justification by grace alone, the believer does not respond to such 'evangelical' sentences [of Scripture] by more penitence, but with thanksgiving."[11] Taken together, the prayer is making a statement about the cleansing nature of the Holy Eucharist and the grace that it imparts to the communicant. We eat the flesh and drink the blood of Jesus, which results in our washing and being made clean. That the Holy Eucharist was instituted in both kinds, the Body of Christ for our bodies and the Blood of Christ for our souls, was commonly accepted in the Middle Ages. It is an acknowledgment that each human being is made of both a body and a soul, captured well by the apostle Paul in his first letter to the Thessalonians: "Now may the God of peace himself sanctify you completely, and may your whole spirit and soul and body be kept blameless at the coming of our Lord Jesus Christ" (5:23). Thus, the aid that God provides us, by way of his grace, needs to help both our soul and our body. The prayer affirms that the body and blood of Christ together sanctify our

10. Badie, "Prayer of Humble Access," 110.

11. Badie, "Prayer of Humble Access," 105.

entire being—body and soul: may "the very God of peace sanctify you wholly," as the apostle says.

When we pray the "Prayer of Humble Access" we are making petition of humble thankfulness for the work that God has done for us in his once-for-all sacrifice of himself on the cross and also for the ongoing work he is doing in us (soul) and to us (body) by his gift of sanctifying grace that comes through partaking of his body and his blood. We are being made truly whole so whether our sins arise from our inner self (e.g., pride and anger) or as a result of our embodiment (e.g., gluttony and lust) the sanctifying work of the Holy Eucharist is making us not only whole but holy. And it is in this way that the Holy Eucharist is the "source and summit" of our Christian life.

The Spirituality of the Holy Eucharist

The spirituality of the Holy Eucharist, however, is perhaps best summed up in George Herbert's (d. 1633) "The Holy Communion." He writes,

> Not in rich furniture, or fine array,
>   Nor in a wedge of gold,
>   Thou, who from me was sold,
>   To me dost now thyself convey;
> For so thou should'st without me still have been,
>   Leaving within me sin:
>
> But by the way of nourishment and strength,
>   Thou creep'st into my breast;
>   Making thy way my rest,
>   And thy small quantities my length;
> Which spread their forces into every part,
>   Meeting sins force and art.
>
> Yet can these not get over to my soul,
>   Leaping the wall that parts
>   Our souls and fleshly hearts;
>   But as th' outworks, they may control

My rebel-flesh, and carrying thy name,
    Affright both sin and shame.

Only thy grace, which with these elements comes,
    Knows the ready way,
    And hath the privy key,
Op'ning the soul's most subtle rooms:
While those to spirits refin'd, at door attend
    Dispatches from their friend.

Give me my captive soul, or take
    My body also thither.
Another lift like this will make
    Them both to be together.

Before that sin turn'd flesh to stone,
    And all our lump to leaven;
A fervent sigh might well have blown
    Our innocent earth to heaven.

For sure when Adam did not know
    To sin, or sin to another;
He might to heav'n from Paradise go,
    As from one room t' another.

Thou hast restor'd us to this ease
    By this thy heav'nly blood,
Which I can go to, when I please,
    And leave th' earth to their food.

Perhaps no Anglican priest has had such a profound and affective relationship to the Holy Eucharist as Herbert. In his *A Priest to the Temple*, he writes movingly about the privilege of confecting and conveying the Eucharist:

> The country parson being to administer the Sacraments, is at a stand with himself how or what behavior to assume for so holy things. Especially at Communion times he is in a great confusion, as being not only to receive God, but to break, and administer him. Neither finds he any issue in this, but to throw himself down at the throne

of grace, saying, Lord, thou knowest what thou didst, when thou appointedst it to be done thus; therefore do thou fulfil what thou didst appoint; for thou art not only the feast, but the way to it.[12]

Herbert had a profound sense of his unfitness to be a priest. He "saw the function of a priest in a community in practical terms: primarily spiritual, of course, through teaching, preaching, charity, and the celebration of the sacraments, but extending also to the giving of legal advice and the provision of health care."[13] For Herbert the most essential quality for a priest was a life of holiness, which led him to write his work *A Priest to the Temple; or, The Country Parson, His Character, and Rule of Holy Life.* Throughout his poem "The Priesthood," Herbert speaks of his unworthiness to serve as an effective preacher and maker of the Holy Eucharist. He concludes,

Wherefore I dare not, I, put forth my hand
To hold the Ark, although it seems to shake[14]
Through th' old sins and new doctrines of our land.
Only, since God doth often vessels make
Of lowly matter for high uses meet,
     I throw me at his feet.
There will I lie, until my Maker seek
For some mean stuff thereon to show his skill:
Then is my time. The distance of the meek
Doth flatter power. Lest good come short of ill
In praising might, the poor do by submission
     What pride by opposition.[15]

How fitting then that he should write about the Holy Eucharist with such beauty, theological nuance, and spiritual sensitivity.

In the first stanza of "The Holy Communion," Herbert speaks to the simple and humble, even earthly, elements of bread and wine. This ordinary food and drink are not "a wedge of gold" or anything bearing "fine array" but simple bread and wine. It is Jesus

12. "A Priest to the Temple" 22, in Herbert, *Complete English Poems*, 232.

13. Wilcox, "Herbert, George."

14. See 2 Sam 6:3–8 or 1 Chr 13:7–11.

15. Herbert, *Complete English Poems*, 152.

who gives himself to us as the Great High Priest ("thyself convey"), for the priest stands at the altar only as an *alter Christus* celebrating *in persona Christi*. We, sinful human beings in the lineage of Adam, "sold" Christ by our sin. Without his self-offering of himself for the sins of the world there would still be the stain of original sin within us ("Leaving within me sin"). The way that the Holy Eucharist deals with sin is the subject of the second verse. Picking up language from Cranmer, Herbert speaks of the "nourishment and strength" that creeps into his breast, which brings him rest from the unrest of sin. These "small quantities" of bread and wine "spread their forces into every part, Meeting sins force and art." The grace that comes by way of the Holy Eucharist, which nourishes and strengthens, easily conquers the results of original sin.

It can also defeat our everyday sins if, and only if, it can leap "the wall that parts Our souls and fleshly heart." The image here is that the literal bread and wine, consumed by my body, contains the spiritual body and blood of Jesus Christ so the material elements of bread and wine need not only to nourish us physically but nourish us spiritually as well. In the words of Cranmer, "For as there is a carnal generation, and a carnal feeding and nourishment, so is there also a spiritual generation, and a spiritual feeding. . . . And as every man is carnally fed and nourished in his body by meat and drink, even so is every good Christian man spiritually fed and nourished in his soul by the flesh and blood of our Saviour Christ."[16] If, and when, the spiritual food and the grace of the Eucharist makes its way into our soul, our "rebel-flesh" is put under "control." Further, the work of grace in the soul then affrights subsequent "sin and shame" from rearing its ugly head. There is here a true deliverance from sin and shame: "As far as the east is from the west, so far does he remove our transgressions from us" (Ps 103:12). In the words of the BCP 1549's order for the "Visitation of the Sick": "O most merciful God, which according to the multitude of thy mercies, doest so put away the sins of those which truly repent, that thou remembrest them no more."

16. Cranmer, *Defensio verae et catholicae doctrinae de sacramento* 1.10, in Cranmer, *Archbishop Cranmer*, 16.

Herbert's fourth stanza becomes even more explicit with its acknowledgment that only God's grace, "which with these elements comes, Knows the ready way, And hath the privy key," opens "the soul's most subtle rooms." Grace knows the way, it knows how to open the inner person to the mysterious working of God. For Cranmer, the change effected by the Holy Eucharist is within us: "all the alteration is inwardly and spiritually."[17] Further, the grace of the Holy Eucharist has the "privy key." "Privy" here means more than just private, for the grace of the Eucharist is not private but public, available to any baptized Christian who eats and drinks worthily (cf. 1 Cor 11:27–29). Rather, "privy" is something that belongs to a particular person, something that is reserved for the exclusive use of that person. That is, if each person is a locked door, then God fashions, by grace, a key that is unique to that person; and this key is able to unlock the unique lock. God's grace is individualized, if you will, so that each of us receives God's proper ministrations. These unique keys are "Op'ning the soul's most subtle rooms." The rooms of our soul are subtle because they are cleverly made and designed because each of us is unique, requiring a unique key to open them. All the while, Christ is speaking within the soul, sending messages to the physical elements of bread and wine: "While those to spirits refin'd, at door attend Dispatches from their friend." There is a rich theological insight here that we need to note: Christ is not only present to us in the bread and the wine but he is also present in us so that he can speak to our soul regarding the grace of the Eucharist. Herbert is not clear as to how Christ is so powerfully present. Similarly, Jeremy Taylor (d. 1667), Herbert's contemporary, writes in his *Holy Living*, "Dispute not concerning the secret of the mystery, and the nicety of the manner of Christ's presence: it is sufficient to thee that Christ shall be present to thy soul, as an instrument of grace."[18] It is best to let the mysteries of God remain a mystery!

17. Cranmer, *Defensio verae et catholicae doctrinae de sacramento* 2.5, in Cranmer, *Archbishop Cranmer*, 49, summarizing the thought of Eusebius Emissenus (d. ca. 359).

18. Taylor, *Holy Living* 4.10, in Taylor, *Jeremy Taylor* (ed. Stanwood), 259.

This then leads Herbert to shift his focus a bit in the second half of the poem. He begins by asking God to give him back his captive soul or to take his soul and body together into his presence. Herbert's enthusiasm for receiving the Eucharist and the grace that comes thereby assures him that God will "lift . . . Them both to be together." Sin, which "turn'd flesh to stone," makes the Eucharist and grace necessary. Before sin a "fervent sigh" was enough to "have blown Our innocent earth to heaven." That is, in a state of innocence not only would humankind have been able to walk with God "in the garden in the cool of the day" (Gen 3:8) but sinless man would have been able to flit between "Paradise" and heaven as "from one t'another." But sin erected a wall between us and God, a wall that the death and resurrection of Jesus "has broken down" (Eph 2:14) and a wall that is easily overcome by the grace of the Holy Eucharist. "Thou hast restor'd us to this ease By this thy heav'nly blood, Which I can go to, when I please," writes Herbert, "And leave th' earth to their food." Thus, "the easy passage promised by the [Eucharistic] elements' possession of the key to his soul through grace described at the end of the first part is matched by the sacramental power of the Communion" so that "the message of the second half [of the poem] parallels God's grace in the first half."[19]

So, let us take a step back from this close reading of the poem and summarize Herbert's understanding of the Eucharist and how this affects our understanding of Anglican spirituality. First, the humble elements of bread and wine betray the great riches of the Eucharistic feast but also serve as an image for us of our own need to come to the Lord's Table humbly. The humble nature of the elements themselves are reflected in the priest's prayer over the offering, which goes back to Jewish practice: "Blessed be though, Yahweh [sic], our God, King of the universe, who givest us this fruit of the vine"; and "Blessed be thou, Yahweh [sic], our God, King of the universe, who bringest forth bread from the earth."[20] Or, in modern Christian parlance, "Blessed are you, Lord God of all creation, for through your goodness we have received the bread we offer you:

19. Whitlock, "Sacramental Poetry," 48.
20. Bouyer, *Eucharist*, 70–80.

fruit of the earth and work of human hands, it will become for us the bread of life"; and "Blessed are you, Lord God of all creation, for through your goodness we have received this wine we offer you: fruit of the vine and work of human hands, it will become our spiritual drink." Through the very common elements of bread and wine God works his Eucharistic miracle. We must, however, receive in a worthy manner, which must include, among other things, humility in imitation of Jesus who "humbled himself by becoming obedient to the point of death, even death on a cross" (Phil 2:8). In the words of Cranmer, we "ought . . . to approach to this heavenly table with all humbleness of heart, and godliness of mind."[21]

Second, and very obviously, we are sinners before God in that we are born in original sin and continue to offend against God by our actual sins. Nonetheless, "as in Adam all die, so also in Christ shall all be made alive" (1 Cor 15:22) for the sacramental grace makes its way through every part of my person: inwardly in my soul and outwardly in my body. It transforms my whole person, for God cares about our souls and bodies: "Grant us therefore, gracious Lord, so to eat the flesh of thy dear Son Jesus Christ, and to drink his blood, that our sinful bodies may be made clean by his body, and our souls washed through his most precious blood" (BCP 1662). The grace of the sacrament nourishes and strengthens every part of us.

Third, because Christ is spiritually present in the bread and the wine, the division between the body and soul, the material and the immaterial has been overcome, the key that unlocks the door has been used. This is why the immaterial grace of the Eucharist effects a change in my embodied sins and offenses. And this is made possible, of course, by the fact that Jesus is both a man and God. The ineffability of the hypostatic union leads to the ineffability of the real presence. It is the incarnation of Jesus Christ at a particular time and in a particular place that is the foundation of all sacramental theology. Without the incarnation there would be no sacramental grace by way of the material bread and wine. Thus,

---

21. Cranmer, *Defensio verae et catholicae doctrinae de sacramento* 4.6, in Cranmer, *Archbishop Cranmer*, 218.

we must encourage frequent Communion so that we continue to receive the grace of God in order to experience the "effectual working of his power" (Eph 3:7 KJV).

Fourth, let us remember that it is by sacramental grace that God has made it possible for us to leave earth for heavenly discourse with God—a movement of *theosis* and union with God. In the words of Edward Pusey (d. 1882):

> The gift vouchsafed in the Holy Communion must be altogether of a different kind, because it is not the stirring up of the human spirit, but the union of the Divine, the Presence of the Redeemer within the soul, when the soul is silent, not acting upon itself, but "caught up," present with its Lord, because "one with Him," penetrated with Him and His Divinity, when in solemn words which have been used, the soul is "transfigured" by His Holy Presence in it.[22]

In short, in receiving Christ's body sacramentally, we receive into our bodies Christ's life and divinity that leads to our own transformation or *theosis*. Further, Pusey says that Christ's "life . . . is transmitted to us also, and not to our souls only, but our bodies also, since we become flesh of His flesh, and bone of His bone."[23] Through Eucharistic grace we are "caught up within the influence of the mystery of [God's] ineffable love."[24] It is by sacramental grace that we are not only brought into a saving relationship with Jesus Christ, but we are made one with the Holy Trinity—as we grow in love we are joined to God who is Love for anyone "who does not love does not know God, because God is love" (1 John 4:8).

---

22. Pusey, *Letter*, 155–56.
23. Pusey, *Holy Eucharist*, 11.
24. Pusey, *Holy Eucharist*, 14.

4

Private Devotion

THE THIRD AREA OF the Anglican spiritual trinity is private devotion. But we need to start with a description of what this is
not. The trajectory of Christian spirituality has been mapped out
many times and it is clear that it was only in the modern period,
somewhere in the seventeenth and eighteenth centuries, that
Christian spiritual traditions became overly, perhaps even overtly,
individualistic. I say "overly" because the nature of the Christian's
relationship to God is, of course, to some degree individual and
personal; that is, a particular person gets baptized, a unique person
is illuminated by the Holy Spirit, a single person receives the Holy
Eucharist and the corresponding sacramental grace, etc. However,
there is a difference between an individual*istic* spirituality and an
individual, personal spirituality that is mediated by the church.
Anglican spirituality is of the latter sort—it concerns the person
(you, me, etc.), but it only understands the person by way of his or
her relationship to the church universal.

Many of us are likely familiar with a kind of Christianity that
reduces everything to a "me and God" mentality: I asked Jesus into
my heart on this day, at this time; Jesus is *my* best friend, or worse,
my "lover"; God spoke to *me* so I am going to do what he tells *me*

to do; I don't need to go to a local church because *I* can commune with God anywhere at any time; etc. Historically, this perspective arises out of Puritanism and Pietism, movements that in and of themselves did much good, but when taken to extremes reduced the body of Christ (i.e., the corporate people of God, the church) to a sociological category that one can take or leave on a whim. This is *not* what we mean when we talk about private devotion.

As is well known, Anglicanism is a corporate expression of the Christian faith.[1] One only has to think of the Book of *Common* Prayer (BCP) wherein all practicing Anglicans are, ideally, saying the same prayers and reading the same Scriptures on the same days at the same time. Our Daily Office and Eucharistic lectionaries allow us to recount salvation history together, even if one is praying Morning Prayer alone. It is "Let *us* humbly confess our sins unto Almighty God" and it is "Almighty God, unto whom all hearts are open, all desires known, and from whom no secrets are hid; Cleanse the thoughts of *our* hearts by the inspiration of thy Holy Spirit, that *we* may perfectly love thee, and worthily magnify thy holy Name" (BCP 1928). In Anglican faith and practice it is always a "we," rarely an "I." So, then, what do we mean when we speak of private devotion?

Private Devotion as Asceticism

In Anglicanism, the most well-known use of the phrase "private devotion" is in Lancelot Andrewes' (d. 1626) *Preces Privatae*, which literally means *Private Prayers*, but is often translated as "The Private Devotions." In this influential work of Anglican spirituality, Andrewes translated into English for the non-Greek-reading, non-Latin-reading Christian a set of prayers and devotions from the catholic Christian tradition that had come down to his time. The text contains prayers to complement the BCP's office for Morning and Evening Prayer and even a "Course of Prayers for the Week." But perhaps what gives us insight into the nature of

---

1. Ross, *Hearing Confessions*, 93.

private devotions is in the rest of the work and I want to focus on several of Andrewes' sections as illustrative: "Additional Exercises" and "The Seven Works of Mercy."

The word "exercises" has a rich history in the Christian spiritual tradition, with the most well-known use of the term coming from sixteenth-century Spain, in the form of Ignatius of Loyola's (d. 1556) *Spiritual Exercises.* Yet, the Christian tradition inherited and, we might say, baptized the concept of exercises from ancient Greek and Roman philosophy. The great scholar of ancient philosophy Pierre Hadot (d. 2010) once said, "Ignatius' *Exercitia spiritualia* are nothing but a Christian version of the Greco-Roman tradition." He goes on to argue that the concept of *askesis* "must be understood not as asceticism, but as the practice of spiritual exercises."[2] Let us assume that Hadot is correct, and therefore view the concept of "exercises" through a philosophical lens before looking at it theologically.

In the ancient world, philosophy was conceived as an art directed toward the cultivation of an ideal disposition of the soul, a disposition that may be called excellence or virtue or wisdom. The subject matter of this art is one's soul and its goal is to transform or to take care of one's soul. The product will be the transformed disposition of the soul, namely excellence or wisdom and this transformed disposition will necessarily impact a person's behavior, expressing itself in actions. That is, this art is concerned with one's life, that *this* is the subject matter, and that its goal is to transform one's life. In other words, the product of this art will be the actions that constitute one's life, highlighting its status as a performative/ practical art.

Central to this conception of philosophy as an art are the roles played by *logos* and *askesis*. In the technical conception of philosophy, the study of philosophical arguments, theories and doctrines is the first part of a philosophical education. Once these are mastered there is then a period of practical training (*askesis*) in which the material of the first part is digested in order to produce the actions or product appropriate to their art. For example,

2. Hadot, *Philosophy*, 82.

a shoemaker can explain how he makes shoes but his primary job (*askesis*) is to make shoes = a shoemaking way of life. Accordingly, philosophy is primarily expressed in actions rather than words, so the best way to uncover someone's philosophical position will be by an examination of her life. This conception of philosophy produces three main types of texts:

> 1) Literature concerned with actions, such as biographical literature and anecdotal material (= saint's lives and sayings of the desert mothers and fathers);
>
> 2) Literature concerned with arguments and doctrine, such as theoretical treatises and commentaries (= theology and scriptural commentary);
>
> 3) Literature concerned with spiritual exercises (*askesis*), such as texts for guiding spiritual exercises and texts written as exercises (= Ignatius of Loyola's *Spiritual Exercises* and other spiritual theology texts).[3]

We can now say the same thing theologically, using much of the same language. Theology is conceived as an art directed toward the cultivation of an ideal disposition of the soul, a disposition that may be called virtue, wisdom, or holiness. The subject matter of this art is one's soul and its goal is to transform or to take care of one's soul. The product will be the transformed disposition of the soul, namely virtue, wisdom, or holiness, and this transformed disposition will necessarily impact a person's behavior, expressing itself in actions. That is, this art of theology is concerned with one's spiritual life, that *this* is the subject matter, and that its goal is to transform one's life. In other words, the product of this art will be the actions that constitute one's life, highlighting its status as a practical art. Central to this conception of theology as an art are the roles played by *logos* and *askesis*. In the technical conception of theology, the study of the Sacred Scriptures and the doctrines that derive therefrom are the first part of a theological education. Once these are mastered there is then a period of practical training in which the material of the first part is digested in order to produce the actions

---

3. See Sellars, *Art of Living.*

or product appropriate to their art. In short, spiritual exercises are the actions that result from our reading, meditation, and contemplation of the Holy Scriptures and reflection on Christian theology. Thus, they are a natural outgrowth of the Daily Office and the Holy Eucharist. It is not a matter of whether or not we will engage in spiritual exercises but, rather, a question of which ones.

There are perhaps the more obvious and/or biblical ones (e.g., fasting, solitude, meditation, and self-examination) but then there are ones that we are led to do based on discernment and/or under the guidance of a spiritual director. Again, these ascetical actions (i.e., private devotions) grow out of our reading, meditation, and contemplation of the Holy Scriptures and reflection on Christian theology so that our theology will be expressed in actions rather than words. Let us return to Andrewes and use the so-called seven works of mercy as an example of ascetical theology and discipline; or, in simple terms, private devotion.

The concept of the works of mercy goes back to Jesus' teaching in Matt 25:41–46:

> Then he will say to those on his left, "Depart from me, you cursed, into the eternal fire prepared for the devil and his angels. For I was hungry and you gave me no food, I was thirsty and you gave me no drink, I was a stranger and you did not welcome me, naked and you did not clothe me, sick and in prison and you did not visit me." Then they also will answer, saying, "Lord, when did we see you hungry or thirsty or a stranger or naked or sick or in prison, and did not minister to you?" Then he will answer them, saying, "Truly, I say to you, as you did not do it to one of the least of these, you did not do it to me." And these will go away into eternal punishment, but the righteous into eternal life.

In short, to be Christians Jesus' followers are to attend to their inner spiritual lives through outward, physical actions, which in time came to be called the works of mercy, of which there are traditionally seven:

- Feed the hungry

- Clothe the naked

- Give drink to the thirsty

- Shelter the homeless

- Visit the sick

- Ransom the captive

- Bury the dead

Moreover, Thomas Aquinas (d. 1274) understood mercy as "the compassion in our hearts for another person's misery, a compassion which drives us to do what we can to help him."[4] The internal pity that we have for another person Thomas calls "affective," but the action resulting from this pity he terms "effective." Thus, the works of mercy are effective pity and issue forth from our inner affectivity. Andrewes divides the works of mercy up slightly differently, grouping them under two kinds: corporeal and spiritual. The corporeal works are: "Visit: give drink: give meat: redeem the slave: Clothe: tend the sick: and lay the dead in [the] grave." In other words, the corporeal works are the traditional works of mercy. The spiritual works are: "Counsel: rebuke: instruct in wisdom's way: Console: forgive: Endure unmov'd: and pray."[5] Andrewes sees both of these kinds of merciful works issuing forth from one's life of prayer and worship. They are the fruit of the Daily Office and Holy Eucharist.

The common element in all areas of private devotion is that they are forms of asceticism wherein we "exercise self-control in all things" in order not "to receive a perishable wreath, but . . . an imperishable one," as the apostle Paul writes in 1 Cor 9:25. Richard Finn defines asceticism as "voluntary abstention for religious reasons from food and drink, sleep, wealth, or sexual activity. Such abstention may be periodic or permanent."[6] This gets at the

---

4. Aquinas, *Summa theologica* II-II.30.1.

5. *Private Devotions*, 157–58.

6. Finn, *Asceticism*, 1.

heart of asceticism—that it is an abstention. As we have seen, asceticism is not uniquely Christian, but what gives asceticism a specific Christian connotation is that it is an abstention *for a particular end,* such as union with God or to cultivate charity.[7] The late Eastern Orthodox theologian Kallistos Ware (d. 2022) says it well when he writes,

> Asceticism . . . leads us to self-mastery and enables us to fulfill the purpose that we have set for ourselves, whatever that may be. A certain measure of ascetic self-denial is thus a necessary element in all that we undertake, whether in athletics or politics, in scholarly research or in prayer. Without this ascetic concentration of effort we are at the mercy of exterior forces, or of our own emotions and moods; we are reacting rather than acting. Only the ascetic is inwardly free.[8]

This places Christian asceticism "in a wholly positive light. It is an essential component of spiritual growth analogous to the athlete's quest to achieve peak physical efficiency."[9]

Ware makes a distinction between natural asceticism and unnatural asceticism: "Natural asceticism reduces material life to the utmost simplicity, restricting our physical needs to a minimum, but not maiming the body or otherwise deliberately causing it to suffer. Unnatural asceticism, on the other hand, seeks out special forms of mortification that torment the body and gratuitously inflict pain upon it."[10] Thus, in Ware's examples, to wear cheap and simple clothing is natural asceticism whereas wearing hair shirts and fetters with iron spikes piercing the body is unnatural. Similarly, it is natural asceticism to sleep on the floor but unnatural asceticism to sleep on a bed of nails; natural to live in a cave versus

---

7. See de Guibert, "La notion d'ascèse, d'ascétisme," 937.

8. Kallistos Ware, "The Way of the Ascetics: Negative or Affirmative?," in Wimbush and Valantasis, eds., *Asceticism*, 3.

9. Luke Dysinger, "Asceticism and Mystical Theology," in Howells and McIntosh, eds., *Oxford Handbook*, 165.

10. Kallistos Ware, "The Way of the Ascetics: Negative or Affirmative?," in Wimbush and Valantasis, eds., *Asceticism*, 9–10.

a nice house but unnatural to stand permanently on a pillar; natural to refrain from marriage and sexual activity but unnatural to castrate oneself; and natural to eat only vegetables and not meat, drink water and not wine, but unnatural to make our food and drink repulsive.

Moreover,

> unnatural asceticism, in other words, evinces either explicitly or implicitly a distinct hatred for God's creation, and particularly for the body; natural asceticism may do this, but on the whole it does not. The official attitude of the church, especially from the fourth century onwards, has been entirely clear. Voluntary abstinence for ascetic reasons is entirely legitimate; but to abstain out of a loathing for the material creation is heretical.[11]

Asceticism that reduces one's needs to a minimum in order to provide greater self-sufficiency for holy living is to be favored over excessive and/or feigned self-control. Or, to say it in slightly different terms, better the ascetic be frugal and simple than to be luxurious and extravagant. Thus, asceticism, as an essential component of spiritual growth, is the voluntary abstention from the lesser goods of this life (for a period of time or permanently) for the purpose of maintaining inner attentiveness to God and achieving union with God.

George Herbert's "Lent" as Ascetical Theology

I would like to end by returning to one of my favorite Anglican theologians, George Herbert, and his poem "Lent":

> Welcome dear feast of Lent: who loves not thee,
> He loves not Temperance, or Authority,
> But is composed of passion.
> The Scriptures bid us *fast*; the Church says, *now*:
> Give to thy Mother, what thou wouldst allow
> To every Corporation.

11. Kallistos Ware, "The Way of the Ascetics: Negative or Affirmative?," in Wimbush and Valantasis, eds., *Asceticism*, 10.

The humble soul composed of love and fear
Begins at home, and lays the burden there,
    When doctrines disagree.
He says, in things which use hath justly got,
I am a scandal to the Church, and not
    The Church is so to me.
True Christians should be glad of an occasion
To use their temperance, seeking no evasion,
    When good is seasonable;
Unless Authority, which should increase
The obligation in us, make it less,
    And Power itself disable.
Besides the cleanness of sweet abstinence,
Quick thoughts and motions at a small expense,
    A face not fearing light:
Whereas in fullness there are sluttish fumes,
Sour exhalations, and dishonest rheumes,
    Revenging the delight.
Then those same pendant profits, which the spring
And Easter intimate, enlarge the thing,
    And goodness of the deed.
Neither ought other men's abuse of Lent
Spoil the good use; lest by that argument
    We forfeit all our Creed.
It's true, we cannot reach Christ's fortieth day;
Yet to go part of that religious way,
    Is better than to rest:
We cannot reach our Savior's purity;
Yet are bid, *Be holy even as he.*
    In both let's do our best.
Who goes in the way which Christ hath gone,
Is much more sure to meet with him, than one
    That travelleth by-ways:
Perhaps my God, though he be far before,
May turn, and take me by the hand, and more
    May strengthen my decays.

Yet Lord instruct us to improve our fast
By starving sin and taking such repast
    As may our faults control:

> That every man may revel at his door,
> Not in his parlor; banqueting the poor,
>   And among those his soul.

There are several things to notice here. First, when the church legislates acts of mortification and asceticism we should, as part of our private devotion, which is corporate in nature, submit ourselves to the church's wisdom and do those things that she asks of us, such as the full regimen of fast days as legislated in the BCP. Second, "True Christians" are "glad . . . To use their temperance" at all times, but especially at those times legislated by the authority of the church. Third, proper asceticism is "sweet" and leads to "cleanness" in our spiritual lives. Fourth, though we will never be as holy as Jesus we should at least try to be: "It's true, we cannot reach Christ's fortieth day; Yet to go part of that religious way, Is better than to rest." Fifth, following the example of Christ, walking in *via Christi*, is a more sure guarantee of becoming like Jesus. Sixth and lastly, the nature of asceticism, as we have seen, is a lack of something for a greater good, a "starving" of sin, in the words of Herbert.

So, Anglican Christians should be practitioners of private devotions, and athletes of asceticism. Anglican Christians should embrace a full Anglican spirituality, in all of its trinitarian fullness, praying faithfully the Divine Office, partaking regularly of the body and blood of Christ and practicing those corporeal and spiritual works of mercy, done for the good of the church and to the glory of God.

5

Anglican Spirituality and Mission

OVER THE CENTURIES THE collective nature of the Christian faith has eroded into an unhealthy individualism.[1] As mentioned in chapters 1 and 4, Anglican spirituality attempts to resist this modern tendency by striving to keep a balance between the corporate and the individual and the subjective and the objective. But now that we have distilled the threefold rule of Anglican spirituality, it is worth returning to this issue. Does Anglican spirituality adequately maintain a proper focus on the corporate and objective or does it, following the general trend in modern Christianity, lend itself to an unhealthy individualistic practice of the faith? Or, to ask the question differently, does Anglican spirituality contribute to the building up of the catholicity of the Christian faith? Does Anglican spirituality enable the church to accomplish her divine mission? If Anglican spirituality only tends toward individualism then it is *not* maintaining a proper balance between the corporate and individual. On the other hand, if it does not form the individual Christian as an individual then it has swung too far in the corporate direction. Like so many theological foci, the proper balance lies in the middle, a kind of Aristotelian theological mean, if you will.

1. See Trueman, *Rise and Triumph*.

Individualism and the Corporate Nature of the Church

It is true that much of the Christian tradition has focused on the individual, but not at the expense of the corporate. The way that the church has done this historically is through a focus on interiority. Romans 12:2, for example, admonishes the believer to "not be conformed to this world, but be transformed by the renewal of your mind, that by testing you may discern what is the will of God, what is good and acceptable and perfect." Notice that the transformation comes about by the renewal of one's mind—there is the need for the *individual* to be transformed. The language of "mind" here is *nous*, which is the intellectual faculty or the highest faculty that allows one to perceive divine things. An individual needs to be renewed in her mind so that she can "discern the will of God." The process and practices that lead to this individual transformation, however, are corporate: the Daily Office and the Holy Eucharist, for example. The data that renews one's mind must come from outside oneself but it must be interiorized, made applicable to each individual by each individual. The language of the Collect for the Second Sunday of Advent discussed above again serves as an example, for it is in hearing, reading, marking, and learning the Holy Scriptures that we are enabled to "inwardly digest them." A similar interiority is found in the third of the BCP 1552 post-Offertory Collects when there is no Communion: "Grant, we beseech thee, Almighty God, that the words which we have heard this day, with our outward ears, may through thy grace be so grafted inwardly in our hearts, that they may bring forth in us the fruit of good living, to the honour and praise of thy name; through Jesus Christ our Lord. Amen." To use the language of Augustine of Hippo, we must move *intra se* (into ourselves) before we can move *extra se* (outside ourselves). The way to God is an interior movement, for God is within each person and he can be found there: "you will know that I am in my Father, and you in me, and I in you" (John 14:20). Thus, the Christian tradition's sense of the individualistic is the necessity of interiority, for God is in us.

Anglicanism inherited from the catholic Christian tradition the tension and need for a proper balance between the individual and the corporate. From the start the Book of Common Prayer (BCP) imagined both an individual and corporate practice of the threefold Anglican rule. In the Preface to the BCP 1552 we read "that all things shall be read and sung in the Church in the English tongue, to the end that the congregation may be thereby edified." The expectation is that there is a congregation, "but when men [sic] say Morning and Evening prayer privately, they may say the same in any language that they themselves do understand." Though the English language is legislated for use because it presumes a congregation of English speakers, the BCP also immediately understands that the offices will, at times, be prayed privately; that is, individually but, of course, communally in the sense that no individual Christian truly prays alone but with all the saints of God, those alive and those in glory. Further, priests and deacons are expected to pray the Daily Office "either privately or openly" (i.e., publicly with others) whereas curates, those responsible for a church or chapel, "shall say the same in the Parish Church or Chapel where he ministereth, and shall toll a bell thereto . . . that such as be disposed may come to hear God's word, and to pray with him." It seems what the BCP envisioned for Anglican faith and practice was the corporate practice of her services except when that was not possible. Where and when possible, pray together. And nothing has changed for Anglicans strive to pray corporately when possible but individually when they cannot pray together. Notice the beginning of the BCP 1928's "Concerning the Service of the Church": "The Order for Holy Communion, the Order for Morning Prayer, the Order for Evening Prayer, and the Litany, as set forth in this Book, are the regular Services appointed for *Public* Worship in this Church, and shall be used accordingly."[2] And it is the corporate nature of Anglican worship and thereby Anglican spirituality that allows it not only to avoid the pitfalls of an unhealthy individualism but equips it for its corporate divine mission.

2. Italics added for emphasis.

From the earliest days of Anglicanism, it was understood that the Holy Eucharist was equipping the communicants for ministry: "we now most humbly beseech thee, O heavenly Father, so to assist us with thy grace, that we may continue in that holy fellowship, and do all such good works as thou has prepared for us to walk in" (BCP 1552). There are three emphases to notice in this Post-Communion prayer: (1) the Holy Eucharist conveys grace; (2) that grace allows the communicants to continue as members of the church; and (3) the church is sent out to do good works. That the Holy Eucharist conveys grace was discussed in chapter 3 (and in the appendix) so I will focus here on the second and third points, using them to develop an Anglican understanding of mission that is empowered by the Daily Office, Holy Eucharist, and private devotion.

The very act of Holy Communion unites individuals with and into the church of Jesus Christ. This reality is reflected in the aforementioned Post-Communion Prayer when the congregation heartily thanks God for feeding them "with the spiritual food of the most precious body and blood" of Jesus Christ, assuring them that they "be very members incorporate in [God's] mystical body, which is the blessed company of all faithful people." At baptism a person is joined to the church: "We receive this Child (Person) into the congregation of Christ's flock" and "this Child (this Person) is regenerate, and grafted into the body of Christ's Church" (BCP 1928). But it is the grace that comes at each and every Holy Eucharist that allows the believer to continue as a member of Christ's church. It is the grace of God sustaining one's faith that knits individual Christians into the body of Christ. It is the grace of God that sustains the Christian community so that it can do the work that God has given it to do. And what is that work? In the words of the BCP, it is the "good works" God "prepared for [the church] to walk in." Given the symmetry of the Eucharistic liturgy, it seems reasonable to conclude that the "good works," at a minimum, include loving God with all of one's heart, soul, and mind and loving one's neighbor as oneself; or, in the words of Homily 6, "A Sermon of Christian Love and Charity," written by the Bishop of London Edmund Bonner (d. 1569) and included in the *First Book of Homilies*, "Charity is to love God with all our heart, all our life and all our powers and strength."[3]

Beginning with the BCP 1552, the Eucharistic liturgy began with the recitation of the Collect for Purity, followed by the saying of the Ten Commandments with "the people kneeling" and responding, after each Commandment, "Lord, have mercy upon us, and incline our hearts to keep this law." Why this practice of saying the Ten Commandments was introduced into the prayer book is unclear,[4] but it remained in the 1662 revision, albeit altered so that the minister turns toward the congregation instead of the altar while rehearsing them. It was only in the eighteenth century that the recitation of the full Ten Commandments could be replaced with the Summary of the Law, like that from Matt 22:37–39. The purpose of the Ten Commandments at the beginning of the liturgy was likely included by Thomas Cranmer for "the advancement of godliness," to use his language from the Preface to the BCP 1552. And what is godliness if not to love God wholly and to love our neighbor as ourselves? Bonner puts it this way, "charity is also to love every man [*sic*], good and evil, friend and foe, and whatsoever cause be given to the contrary, yet nevertheless to bear good will and heart unto every man, to use ourselves well unto them as well in words and countenance as in all our outward acts and deeds."[5] Thus, when at the end of the service the church prays to do "good works" as a result of God's grace, she is praying for the ability to love God and neighbor entirely. And this prayer would be consistent with the Christian tradition's emphasis on God as Love (cf. 1 John 4:8), therefore, to love him is the highest degree of good works.[6]

3. Bray, ed., *Books of Homilies*, 53.

4. It may have been due to the influence of the Lutheran practice that Cranmer experienced during his time in Germany in the 1530s. The Lutherans had replaced the *Confietor* ("I confess") to the saints with the Decalogue in their revision of the Roman rite. It could also have been the result of the Strasbourg reformer Martin Bucer's (d. 1551) influence, for he had settled in Cambridge, England at the time of Cranmer's revision. I am thankful to the Rev. Steve Macias for pointing this out to me.

5. Bray, ed., *Books of Homilies*, 53.

6. See, for example, Bernard of Clairvaux's *On Loving God* or Thomas Traherne's *Centuries of Meditation*.

The Church's Mission

But it also seems reasonable to think that the good works that the church has been prepared to walk in must also refer to the church's divine calling to "make disciples of all nations, baptizing them in the name of the Father and of the Son and of the Holy Spirit, [and] teaching them to observe all that [God has] commanded" (Matt 28:19–20).[7] According to Jesse Zink, "The [Roman] Catholic counter-Reformation produced some of the first missionaries from Europe to other parts of the world. The Reformed impulse of Protestantism, by contrast, acted as a deterrent to Christian mission for many centuries. If God pre-destined people to salvation, then there was little room for human activity in bringing about the salvation of others."[8] This may be true historically, but ensuring that the gospel was brought to sinners was a concern of Anglicans from the start. Cranmer's Collect for Good Friday illustrates this well:

> Merciful God, who hast made all men, and hatest nothing that thou hast made, nor wouldest the death of a sinner, but rather that he should be converted and live: have mercy upon all Jews, Turks, Infidels and Heretics, and take from them all ignorance, hardness of heart, and contempt of thy word. And so fetch them home, blessed Lord, to thy flock, that they may be saved among the remnant of the true Israelites, and be made one fold under one shepherd, Jesus Christ our Lord: who liveth and reigneth. &c. [sic][9]

Cranmer envisioned that the gospel would be spread to other nations so he was clear that the BCP could be adapted in "other nations. . . . For we think it convenient that every country should use such ceremonies, as they shall think best to the setting forth

---

7. This seems to be clear in the BCP 2019's Anglican Standard Text, where the following was added to the Prayers of the People: "Prosper, we pray, all those who proclaim the Gospel of your kingdom throughout the world, and strengthen us to fulfill your great commission, making disciples of all nations, baptizing them and teaching them to obey all that you have commanded."

8. Zink, "Brief Introductions," 446.

9. Ketley, ed., *Two Liturgies*, 247.

of God's honour and glory."[10] Yet "mission" must not be reduced to only "foreign missions" or made synonymous with particular overt forms of evangelism. The divine mission of the church, as given by Matthew, is to make disciples, and that is much richer of an endeavor than just evangelism.[11]

In one sense the whole architecture of the BCP is intended to make disciples. This whole book is suggesting that Anglican spirituality is about disciple-making. But I think that there is a way in which a person can be formed spiritually through the Daily Office, Holy Eucharist, and personal devotion and *not* engage in mission. The congregation prays to be sent out to do God's work, but that does not mean that each person, in fact, does that work. This is the reality of the ongoing nature of the effects of the world, the flesh, and the devil. Hence the need for an intentionality in engaging in God's divine ecclesial mission. Just like a recent communicant may not love God wholly and not love his neighbor as himself, he can also ignore the business of making disciples. Nonetheless, making disciples is the task of the church, it is her God-appointed mission to a fallen and sinful world. And that mission is accomplished through the work of the people of God enabled and empowered by the threefold Anglican rule.

10. Thomas Cranmer, "Of Ceremonies," in the BCP 1549; Ketley, ed., *Two Liturgies*, 157. See also the 39 Articles of Religion's Article 34, "Of the Traditions of the Church": "It is not necessary that traditions and ceremonies be in all places one or utterly alike; for at all times they have been diverse, and may be changed according to the diversity of countries, times, and men's manners, so that nothing be ordained against God's word."

11. In one sense all of the church's activities (e.g., the liturgy) are evangelistic, in that they are done with the purpose of helping people be regenerated and sanctified. For this perspective, see Bevins, *Liturgical Mission*. What I have in mind here is the ministry of actively sharing one's faith through a presentation of the gospel; what is called one-on-one evangelism.

Evangelism and Edification

As I have shown, the fundamental purpose for the church's existence is to make disciples, which is accomplished through two basic means, evangelism and edification:

> And he gave the apostles, the prophets, the evangelists, the shepherds and teachers, to equip the saints for the work of ministry, for building up the body of Christ, until we all attain to the unity of the faith and of the knowledge of the Son of God, to mature manhood, to the measure of the stature of the fullness of Christ, so that we may no longer be children, tossed to and fro by the waves and carried about by every wind of doctrine, by human cunning, by craftiness in deceitful schemes. Rather, speaking the truth in love, we are to grow up in every way into him who is the head, into Christ, from whom the whole body, joined and held together by every joint with which it is equipped, when each part is working properly, makes the body grow so that it builds itself up in love. (Eph 4:11–16)

Simply put, evangelism is the communication of the gospel with the intent of converting the hearer to faith in Jesus Christ and is accomplished through both corporate and individual evangelism, both of which employ a variety of methods. Each parish is responsible to saturate it's communities with love and to demonstrate a unity and oneness (Eph 4:1–3; Col 3:14) that provide the basis for verbal communication and to demonstrate a Christian lifestyle in all human relationships so as to create a basis on which to discuss the life-changing work of Jesus Christ. Edification, the apostle Paul's "building up the body of Christ," is accomplished through the sacraments and the transformation of the believer by the Holy Spirit within the context of the church. Cranmer's "Of Ceremonies" in the BCP 1549 says that the human-made ceremonies used in the church that were devised "of godly intent and purpose" and have not "turned to vanity and supervision" should be retained because they provide "a decent order in the Church . . . because they pertain to edification, whereunto all things done in the Church (as the Apostle teacheth) ought to be referred." Further, these "ceremonies which do serve to a decent order and godly discipline, and such as be apt to stir up the dull mind of man [sic], to the remembrance of his duty to God, by some notable and special signification" are done so that the worshipper "might be edified." The Preface to the BCP 1549 says that the liturgy is read and prayed in English so "that the congregation may be thereby edified."

And there are many places in the BCP where the language is clearly edificatory, even if the word "edification" is not used. For example, at Morning Prayer the officiant reminds the congregation that sin is confessed "to render thanks for the great benefits that we have received at [God's] hands, to set forth his most worthy praise, to hear his most holy Word, and to ask those things that are requisite and necessary, as well for the body as for the soul" (BCP 1662). That is, we pray and hear God's word because it builds us up (Latin *aedificare* = to build), it edifies us. One way to be edified is to be warned about the dangers of approaching God in an unholy or unworthy manner, like that included in the exhortation prior to Communion: the apostle Paul "exhorteth all persons diligently to try and examine themselves, before they presume to eat of that bread and drink of that cup: for as the benefit is great, if with a truly penitent heart, and lively faith, we receive that holy Sacrament . . . so is the danger great, if we receive the same unworthily" (BCP 1549). Likewise, the communicant should recall "the innumerable benefits, which . . . [Jesus Christ] hath obtained to us, he hath left in those holy mysteries, as a pledge of his love, and a continual remembrance of the same, his own blessed body, and precious blood, for us to feed upon spiritually, to our endless comfort and consolation" (BCP 1549). Certainly "comfort and consolation" edifies. Lastly, Cranmer's office for the "Visitation of the Sick" in the BCP 1549 is replete with edificatory sentiments for the one who is facing imminent death. The minister exhorts the sick person as follows: "Dearly beloved, know this, that Almighty God is the Lord over life, and death, and over all things to them pertaining, as youth, strength, health, age, weakness, and sickness. Wherefore, whatsoever your sickness is, know you certainly, that it is God's visitation." Though the sickness might be to try the sick person's patience or "to correct and amend . . . whatsoever doth offend the eyes of our heavenly Father," in either case the sickness is "God's visitation." The ill person should then submit herself to God's will and repent of her sins for "it will turn to [her] profit, and help [her] forward in the right way that leadeth unto everlasting life." She should "take therefore in good worth [i.e., as kindly intended] the chastement of the Lord: for whom the Lord loveth he chastiseth" (cf. Heb 12:6). In other words, giving oneself over to God in repentance is evidence of God's love in spite of the cause of one's sickness. All of this brings peace and consolation for "there should be no greater comfort o christian [sic] persons, than to be made like unto Christ, by suffering patiently adversities, troubles, and sicknesses." Even in death the goal of the liturgy is to build up the dying into the likeness of Christ. The purpose is to edify.

We can conclude then that the corporate nature of Anglican spirituality equips the believer to go out and do the work that God has given her to do, which is to love God and neighbor and to evangelize and edify. The Daily Office provides us communion with God through prayer and the Scriptures so that God's Word will be on our lips when we evangelize others. Personal devotion aids our growth in holiness and Christlikeness so that the world will see our good works and give glory to our Father who is in heaven (Matt 5:16). One is reminded of the saying, "Preach the gospel at all times; when necessary, use words," spuriously attributed to Francis of Assisi (d. 1226). We evangelize through word and deed. And the Holy Eucharist gives us the grace necessary to do these good works of love and mission. At the risk of repeating content from chapter 3, Anglicans believe that when we worship, we do so sacramentally; that is, that when we ask the Holy Spirit to come upon the bread and the wine and make them into the body and blood of Jesus Christ that he does so, turning natural things, bread and wine, into supernatural gifts of God. And what makes this action sacramental in particular is that as sacrament they now convey to us grace. In the words of Article 25 they are "effectual signs of grace." Thus, Anglicans hold that the sacraments give the grace needed to live lives pleasing to God. This grace justifies and sanctifies, for it is the nature of supernatural grace to transfigure and transform communicants into the image if Jesus Christ. In short, Anglicans are sacramentalists, believing in the efficacy of the grace of God, for supernatural grace leads to supernatural acts of doing (e.g., loving, evangelizing, and building others up) that are above and beyond the norm in order to be a properly missional church.

Yet grace comes not only from the Holy Eucharist, but also through acts of grace (cf. 2 Cor 8:6). In the Christian tradition these acts of grace are most frequently referred to as the "means of grace" and include such actions as the reading and preaching of the Word of God, fasting, praying, and a host of other means; that is, through actions that are proper to our personal devotion. The gift of grace is not limited only to the Holy Eucharist but comes through other channels. Martin Thornton captures this sentiment well:

> There is a unique channel of grace which is the Church, a channel through which God acts upon his world. . . . By the Incarnation a unique pipeline is established between heaven and earth: the two are linked and at one. And this pipeline extends through the ages as the Church—a pipe through which the crystal purity of God's grace may flow by the unique means of sacraments and worship.[12]

We are empowered by God's grace to go forth into the world to love and serve him. The mission of the church is made possible by the work and grace of God, utilizing the prayers, communions, and spiritual disciplines of the people of God. The church does not fulfill her mission in her own strength but in the empowerment provided by God through his means of grace.

12. Thornton, *Pastoral Theology*, 117–18.

Appendix

Anglican Theological Anthropology
A Case Study in John Donne ————————

THE ANGLICAN POET AND theologian[1] John Donne (d. 1631), in his Divine Meditations 5, describes humanity this way:

> I am a little world made cunningly
> Of elements and an angelic sprite,
> But black sin hath betray'd to endless night
> My world's both parts, and oh both parts must die.
> You which beyond that heaven which was most high
> Have found new spheres, and of new lands can write,
> Pour new seas in mine eyes, that so I might
> Drown my world with my weeping earnestly,
> Or wash it, if it must be drown'd no more.
> But oh it must be burnt; alas the fire
> Of lust and envy have burnt it heretofore,
> And made it fouler; let their flames retire,
> And burn me O Lord, with a fiery zeal
> Of thee and thy house, which doth in eating heal.

1. Tebeaux, "Donne and Hooker," 30: "Hooker is considered the seminal figure, the paradigm, in the statement and development of Anglicanism. Therefore, by comparing Donne's *Sermons* to Hooker's *Laws*, we can discover to what extent Donne adhered to germinating Anglican theology during his ministry, 1615–1631, and in what way Donne may have made any theological contributions."

There are several important things to note in these exquisite lines that give us insight into early Anglican theological anthropology. First, each human is unique in that she is a "little world," a self-contained person capable of feeling and thought, with a body and soul, as we will see, and able to be in communion with her Creator. The use of "cunningly" is deliberate because it also means "artfully," demonstrating that God made humankind with an intentionality and skill, forming us from the primal "elements."

Let us also note, following so much of the Christian tradition (that itself relied on Greek philosophy),[2] Donne says that a human is made up of both body and soul; or, in his words, "of elements and an angelic sprite." The language of "elements" refers to the body, made up of the "stuff," the matter of creation, whereas the "angelic sprite" is the soul.[3] Donne, as an Augustinian, was likely following the theology of Augustine of Hippo (d. 430) who consistently held that a human being was a composite of body and soul. For example, in Augustine's *Literal Meaning of Genesis*, he writes that "the soul is not of a bodily nature . . . but in wonderful ways it is mixed into the body it animates, and with its incorporeal nod, so to say, it powers or steers the body with a kind of concentration, not with any material engine."[4] This Augustinian view passed through Thomas Aquinas, who believed that the soul informs the body as form does matter (*hylomorphism*)[5] and came into Anglicanism explicitly by way of Richard Hooker's (d. 1600) *Laws of Ecclesiastical Polity*.[6] Importantly, it is the soul that makes it pos-

2. Armstrong and Markus, *Christian Faith*.

3. See John Donne, "A Sermon Preached at Whitehall, March 8, 1622": "as soon as my soul enters into heaven, I shall be able to say to the angels, I am of the same stuff as you, spirit and spirit" (see Donne, *Sermons of John Donne*, 46).

4. Augustine, *Literal Meaning of Genesis* 8.21.42, in Augustine, *On Genesis* (trans. Hill), 370.

5. See Aquinas, *Summa theologiae* I, qq. 75–76.

6. See Richard Hooker, *Laws of Ecclesiastical Polity* I.4, 7; Marshall, *Hooker*, 93: Hooker believes that "man is an intellective being—like the angels—but he is also a creature of flesh and blood, a hylomorphic being who has intellect but also has a body and therefore learns by the reflection of his intellect and the testimony of his senses. Man's life is excellent when his human capacities as a

sible for us to be like the angels, to be an "angelic sprite," because it capacitates us with intelligence and the ability to know, to reason. It is this that allows us to know things that are beyond the sensible (e.g., God). Hooker writes, "Goodness is seen with the eye of the understanding. And the light of that eye, is reason,"[7] but because of original sin and the fall, "whereby the instruments being weakened wherewithal the soul (especially in reasoning) doth work, it prefers rest in ignorance before wearisome labour to know."[8]

Returning to Divine Meditation 5, and as previously mentioned, humanity is stained by both original and actual sins ("black sin")[9] that impact both the body and the soul ("betrayed to endless night My world's both parts") so that "both parts must die."[10] That early Anglican theology held a robust theology of original sin is obvious given Article 9 of the 39 Articles of Religion, first published in 1571:

> Original sin stands not in the following of Adam, (as the Pelagians do vainly talk;) but it is the fault and corruption of the Nature of every man, that naturally is engendered of the offspring of Adam; whereby man is very far gone from original righteousness, and is of his own nature inclined to evil, so that the flesh lusts always contrary to the Spirit; and therefore in every person born into this world, it deserves God's wrath and damnation. And this infection of nature doth remain, yea in them that are regenerated; whereby the lust of the flesh, called in Greek, *phronema sarkos*, (which some do expound the wisdom, some sensuality, some the affection, some the desire, of the flesh), is not subject to the Law of God. And although there is no condemnation for them that believe

---

hylomorphic as well as an intellective being are perfected." This is not to claim that Donne was directly dependent on Hooker, but it is possible. See Tebeaux, "Donne and Hooker," 29.

7. Hooker, *Laws of Ecclesiastical Polity* I.4, 2.

8. Hooker, *Laws of Ecclesiastical Polity* I.4, 7.

9. See also Donne's Divine Meditations 4 where he refers to "my black soul."

10. The effects of sin on the body and the soul are prevalent throughout the poetry of Donne. For example, Divine Meditations 1, which says, "Thou hast made me, and shall thy work decay? Repair me now."

and are baptized; yet the Apostle doth confess, that concupiscence and lust hath of itself the nature of sin.

Notice here the reference to original sin that then causes one to be
"inclined to evil," committing actual sins. Though made unique
and singular, endowed with a body and a soul, humans are now
born into sin and worthy of "wrath and damnation" unless "regenerated." For Donne, sin is a "malignant force" that "lessens the
power of [our] natural faculties."[11] Apart from grace we cannot
accomplish anything spiritual and our full deliverance from sin is
eschatological: God "will give you grace, and temporal blessings
too: he will refresh and re-establish your natural faculties, and give
you supernatural faculties. . . . But though all this be already done
. . . though the act of our redemption be past, the Application is
future," writes Donne in Sermon 142.[12] For Donne, sin blurs our
reason and apart from reason we are unable to strive for natural
perfection, much less supernatural perfection.[13] Sin mars the intellect's ability to know properly, which then causes one to will
wrongly, resulting in sins of the body and soul.

Having noted the nature of sinful humanity, Donne now calls
out to God ("You which beyond that heaven which was most high
Have found new spheres, and of new lands can write") asking him

11. Tebeaux, "Donne and Hooker," 32.

12. John Donne, "Sermon CXLII: A Sermon Preached at Greenwich, April
30, 1615," in Donne, *Works of John Donne* (ed. Alford), V:551. Donne's language of "Application" emphasizes that Christ's work of redemption on the
cross is past, but its application continues into the future and is available to all
believers throughout Christian history. In Donne's time, "application" had the
explicit theological meaning of bringing the benefits of salvation to bear on
the heart of the believer. For example, William Perkins (d. 1602) writes, "*Application*, is when we conceive in our hearts a true persuasion of God's mercy
towards us particularly in the free pardon of all our sins, and for the salvation
of our souls." Perkins, *A godly and learned exposition*, 515; modernized.

13. The language of natural versus supernatural goes back to the earliest
Christian theologians but became a hallmark of Scholastic thinking. In short,
grace not only returns fallen humankind back to its original, prelapsarian
state, which is ours by nature and, therefore, natural, but grace also enables
humanity's ascent to God to see him "face to face" (1 Cor 13:12), which is
above humanity's nature (i.e., *super*natural).

to "pour new seas in mine eyes, that so I might Drown my world with my weeping earnestly, Or wash it, if it must be drown'd no more." In short, Donne is asking God to reflood the earth so that the waters will cleanse him from his sin. The obvious biblical reference here is Genesis 6, and by alluding to it, Donne accomplishes two things. First, he reinforces the point he was just making about the depth of his sinfulness. Donne is likely thinking about Gen 6:5, "And God saw that the wickedness of man was great in the earth, and that every imagination of the thoughts of his heart was only evil continually" (KJV). Donne recognizes that he is evil to his core and that his main occupation in life is to want to sin continually. But secondly, Donne also realizes that one can find "grace in the eyes of the LORD" (Gen 6:8 KJV), just like Noah. The waters of Donne's cleansing flood are not those of the "great deep" or from the "widows of heaven" (Gen 7:11 KJV) but come from his tears of repentance.[14] Donne's request is that God would "drown [his] world," that he would destroy Donne's world so that he will not sin any further. Donne wants another Noahic flood so that God will begin again with "new spheres" and "new lands."

Yet, Donne realizes that God has, in fact, promised never to destroy the world again: "The LORD said in his heart, 'I will never again curse the ground because of man, for the intention of man's heart is evil from his youth. Neither will I ever again strike down every living creature as I have done'" (Gen 8:21). Thus, if God is unwilling to destroy Donne to renew him, then he asks to be washed, a likely reference to baptism, especially considering 1 Pet 3:18–21:

> For Christ also suffered once for sins, the righteous for the unrighteous, that he might bring us to God, being put to death in the flesh but made alive in the spirit, in which he went and proclaimed to the spirits in prison, because they formerly did not obey, when God's patience waited in the days of Noah, while the ark was being prepared, in which a few, that is, eight persons, were brought safely

14. On tears of repentance, see Patton and Hawley, eds., *Holy Tears*; and Hausherr, *Penthos*.

through water. Baptism, which corresponds to this, now
saves you, not as a removal of dirt from the body but
as an appeal to God for a good conscience, through the
resurrection of Jesus Christ.

Donne understands that his deliverance from the stain of original
sin can come by way of baptism; that God can restore him through
a constructive movement, not a destructive one. By way of baptism a person's sinful "dirt" is removed from her body through the
"washing of regeneration" (Titus 3:5) for, in the words of the BCP
1549, "Baptism doeth represent unto us our profession, which is to
follow the example of our Savior Christe, and to be made like unto
him, that as he dyed and rose again for us: so should we (which are
Baptized) die from sin, and rise again unto righteousness, continually mortifying all our evil and corrupt affections, and daily pro-
ceeding in all virtue and godliness of living."

But, as it turns out, neither another Noahic flood (which God
will not grant) nor a baptism of tears can fully restore humanity to
its original state. Donne realizes that the effects of sin and humankind's ongoing propensity to sin need something more than baptism.[15] In this he is in agreement with Article 16 of the 39 Articles
of Religion: "Wherefore the grant of repentance is not to be denied
to such as fall into sin after Baptism. After we have received the
Holy Ghost, we may depart from grace given, and fall into sin, and
by the grace of God we may arise again, and amend our lives." If
one can "rise again" and "amend" one's life after baptism, then how
will that happen? According to Donne, it requires burning ("oh it
must be burnt") since it is a burning that has gotten humankind
into this predicament ("alas the fire Of lust and envy have burnt
it heretofore, And made it fouler"). And not only the burning of
original sin but the "fouler" effects of actual sins.

15. Article 27 of the 39 Articles of Religion lists the following as the effects
of baptism: "grafted into the Church; the promises of the forgiveness of sin,
and of our adoption to be the sons of God by the Holy Ghost, are visibly signed
and sealed, Faith is confirmed, and Grace increased by virtue of prayer unto
God." Notice that there is no mention of the removal of original sin.

Izaak Walton (d. 1683), in his life of Donne, writes that "now the *English Church* had gain'd a second St. *Austine* [i.e., Augustine]."[16] In writing this Walton refers primarily to Donne's conversion, which shared remarkable similarities to Augustine of Hippo's lengthy process of conversion recounted in the *Confessions*. Principally, both men engaged in frequent sexual activity and both men had powerful conversion experiences resulting in a sincere dedication to the church—as bishop of Hippo for Augustine and as dean of St. Paul's Cathedral, London for Donne. Yet, this comment from Walton is also true when one investigates the theologies of both Augustine and Donne. As we have already seen, Donne's theology is clearly Augustinian, he quotes from or alludes to his works more than any other source, and he was influential is helping to establish the Augustinian foundations, and thereby the early church foundations, of seventeenth-century Anglican theology.[17] And here, in Divine Meditation 5, Donne is returning to Augustine's theology of sin.

At the core of Augustine's theology of original sin lies concupiscence, humanity's fundamental problem because of the fall: humankind "was dead in spirit by an act of his own will, and doomed, against his will, to die in body also. Having forsaken eternal life, he was condemned also to eternal death, unless he should be redeemed by grace," he writes in the *City of God*.[18] For the bishop of Hippo, concupiscence "is an absolutely radical, internal dislocation, a catastrophic disagreement with oneself. . . . Its nucleus is an anti-divine disposition of the soul" that "proves eventually to be a comprehensively ruinous disharmony at the core of the person."[19] At times Augustine equates concupiscence with original sin that remains, even after baptism, "in the soul and is still a disorder and a ready . . . cause of sin."[20] Over the course of his life, Augustine

16. Walton, *The lives of Dr. John Donne*, 37.

17. Ettenhuber, *Donne's Augustine*.

18. Augustine, *City of God* 14.15 (trans. Dyson, 612).

19. Peter Burnell, "Concupiscence," in Fitzgerald et al, eds., *Augustine through the Ages*, 224.

20. Burnell, "Concupiscence," in Fitzgerald et al, eds., *Augustine through the Ages*, 224.

came to understand that concupiscence is a disorder of the mind, rooted in the whole person, body and soul. Its presence in the human person is the result of a disordered generation:

> Without any doubt, then, human nature is ashamed of its lust, and deservedly ashamed. For the disobedient nature of his lust, which has entirely subdued the organs of generation to its own urges and snatched them from the power of the will, is enough to show what retribution has been visited upon man for the first disobedience. And it was fitting that this retribution should appear especially in that part of the body which brings about the generation of the very nature that was changed for the worse through that first and great sin. That sin, perpetrated when all mankind existed in one man, brought ruin upon them all; and so no one can be rescued from the toils of that sin, which was punished by God's justice, unless the sin is expiated in each man singly by the grace of God.[21]

This connection between concupiscence and sexual activity, per Walton's account, would have been attractive to Donne, accounting for his language of "the fire of lust."

Like Augustine, Donne understands that a person, affected by concupiscence, does not always will rightly, leading to sin.[22] The ultimate solution to this problem is counterintuitive and paradoxical: one needs to burn the fire away. Lust's connection to burning is an ancient concept,[23] including examples in the Christian Scriptures. Job 31:11–12 says, "For [lusting] is an heinous crime; Yea, it is an iniquity to be punished by the judges. For it is a fire that consumeth to destruction, And would root out all mine increase" (KJV); or 1 Cor 7:9: "But if they cannot exercise self-control, they should marry. For it is better to marry than to burn with passion." Further, Donne says that like lust, envy also burns. The connection

21. Augustine of Hippo, *City of God* 14.20 (trans. Dyson, 620).

22. See Augustine, *On Free Choice of the Will*; and Harrison, *Augustine's Way*.

23. And not only a Christian one: "Thus, a man's pure consciousness is covered by his eternal enemy in the form of lust, which is never satisfied, and which burns like fire." *Bhagavad Gita* 3.39.

between lust and envy is made in the book of James ("Ye lust . . . and desire to have" [Jas 4:2 KJV]), likely accounting for this coupling of sins here in Divine Meditation 5.[24] Donne understands that his sins are rooted in his disordered desires, which burn, accounting for why they cannot be extinguished by tears or baptism. But fire can be fought with fire, but only with a fire that comes from God himself ("let their flames retire, And burn me O Lord, with a fiery zeal").

This "fiery zeal" that burns is a zeal "Of thee and thy house, which doth in eating heal," a reference to Ps 69:9: "For the zeal of thine house hath eaten me up; and the reproaches of them that reproached thee are fallen upon me" (KJV). For Donne the flames of lust and envy are extinguished by consuming the Holy Eucharist, for it is in eating that we are healed, suggesting alongside the "Prayer of Humble Access" that what is in need of healing is both the body and soul by way of the body and blood of the Lord. The "fire" that burns up concupiscence is the body and blood of Christ.[25] Zeal for God's "house"—which is either the church or the individual, or both—means partaking of the Holy Eucharist, and receiving the grace that comes thereby. In this way, what burns up the fires of sinful desire is divine grace.

As an example of early Anglian theological anthropology, we see that John Donne relies heavily on earlier patristic and medieval sources, making his anthropology not only Anglican but Augustinian. This, of course, makes sense given the overwhelming influence of Augustine on all theology after the fifth century. As Denis Janz notes, "Throughout the Middle Ages, the influence of Augustine was so comprehensive and his authority so unassailable that virtually no one would have dared to deny his 'Augustinianism.' Every medieval theologian, at the very least, paid lip-service to the

24. Donne also connects the two in his *Devotions upon Emergent Occasions*: "I never see the fever of lust, of envy, of ambition, by any other light, then the darkness and horror of *Hell* itself." Donne, *Devotions* (ed. Raspa), 9; modernized.

25. Coles, "Matter of Belief," 923.

authority of Augustine."[26] Given Donne's continuity with medieval theology, it is not surprising then that his theology would be so thoroughly Augustinian.[27] Donne was indebted to the Scriptures and patristic and medieval theologians for his theological anthropology, but let us not forget that in his anthropology he was also reflecting on his own inner self, and the way that it burned and sinned against God. Therefore, Donne's "moods, whims, emotions, [and] aspirations, in their infinite complexity and subtlety" must not be disregarded as sources of this theology too.[28] In the end we might say that Donne's theological anthropology is not one born merely from theology books but from the book of life as well, from his need to be burned up by the grace of God.

26. Janz, "Towards a Definition," 117.

27. On Donne's similarities and differences to medieval thought, see Bredvold, "Religious Thought."

28. Bredvold, "Religious Thought," 232.

Bibliography

Anonymous. *The Earliest Life of Gregory the Great by an Anonymous Monk of Whitby*. Translated by Bertram Colgrave. Cambridge: Cambridge University Press, 1968.

Anselm. *Anselm of Canterbury: The Major Works*. Edited by Brian Davies and G. R. Evans. Oxford: Oxford University Press, 1998.

Armstrong, A. H., and R. A. Markus. *Christian Faith and Greek Philosophy*. New York: Sheed and Ward, 1960.

Augustine. *The City of God against the Pagans*. Edited and translated by R. W. Dyson. Cambridge: Cambridge University Press, 1998.

———. *The Greatness of the Soul/The Teacher*. Translated by Jospeh M. Colleran. Westminster, MD: Newman, 1950.

———. *On Christian Teaching*. Translated by R. P. H. Green. Oxford: Oxford University Press, 1997.

———. *On Free Choice of the Will*. Translated by Thomas Williams. Indianapolis: Hackett, 1993.

———. *On Genesis: On Genesis—A Refutation of the Manichees, Unfinished Literal Commentary on Genesis, The Literal Meaning of Genesis*. Translated by Edmund Hill. Hyde Park, NY: New City, 2002.

Avis, Paul. *The Identity of Anglicanism: Essentials of Anglican Ecclesiology*. London: T. & T. Clark, 2007.

Badie, Katie. "The Prayer of Humble Access." *Churchman* 120 (2006) 103–17.

Bernard, G. W. *The Late Medieval English Church: Vitality and Vulnerability before the Break with Rome*. New Haven, CT: Yale University Press, 2012.

Bernard of Clairvaux. *On Loving God*. Translated by Robert Walton. Analytical commentary by Emero Stiegman. Kalamazoo, MI: Cistercian, 1995.

Bevins, Winfield. *Liturgical Mission: The Work of the People for the Life of the World*. Downers Grove, IL: InterVarsity, 2022.

Bonhoeffer, Dietrich. *Life Together*. Translated by John W. Doberstein. San Francisco: Harper & Row, 1954.

Bouyer, Louis. *Eucharist: Theology and Spirituality of the Eucharistic Prayer*. Notre Dame, IN: University of Notre Dame Press, 1968.

Bray, Gerald, ed. *The Books of Homilies: A Critical Edition*. Cambridge: Clarke, 2015.

Bredvold, Louis I. "The Religious Thought of Donne in Relation to Medieval and Later Traditions." In *Studies in Shakespeare, Milton and Donne*, edited by Members of the English Department of the University of Michigan, 191–232. London: Macmillan, 1925.

Carruthers, Mary. *The Book of Memory: A Study of Memory in Medieval Culture*. 2nd ed. Cambridge: Cambridge University Press, 2008.

Cassian, John. *The Conferences*. Translated by Boniface Ramsey. New York: Paulist, 1997.

Clark, James G., ed. *The Religious Orders in Pre-Reformation England*. Woodbridge, UK: Boydell, 2002.

Clement of Alexandria. *Christ the Educator*. Translated by Simon P. Wood. Washington, DC: Catholic University of America Press, 1954.

Coles, Kimberly Anne. "The Matter of Belief in John Donne's Holy Sonnets." *Renaissance Quarterly* 68 (2015) 899–931.

Cranmer, Thomas. *Archbishop Cranmer on the True and Catholic Doctrine and Use of the Sacrament of the Lord's Supper*. Edited by Henry Wace. London: Chas. J. Thynne, 1901.

Cyprian. *The Letters of St. Cyprian of Carthage, Volume IV: Letters 67–82*. Translated by G. W. Clarke. New York: Newman, 1989.

———. *St. Cyprian on the Lord's Prayer*. Translated by Herbert T. Bindley. London: SPCK, 1914.

De Guibert, J. "La notion d'ascèse, d'ascétisme." *Dictionnaire de Spiritualité, Tome I*. Paris: Beauchesne, 1937.

Donne, John. *Devotions upon Emergent Occasions*. Edited by Anthony Raspa. New York: Oxford University Press, 1987.

———. *The Sermons of John Donne, Volume IV*. Edited by George R. Potter and Evelyn M. Simpson. Berkeley: University of California Press, 1962.

———. *The Works of John Donne, D. D., Dean of Saint Paul's, 1621–1631, Volume V*. Edited by Henry Alford. London: John W. Parker, 1839.

Dreyer, Elizabeth A., and Mark S. Burrows, eds. *Minding the Spirit: The Study of Christian Spirituality*. Baltimore: Johns Hopkins University Press, 2005.

Ettenhuber, Katrin. *Donne's Augustine: Renaissance Cultures of Interpretation*. Oxford: Oxford University Press, 2011.

Finn, Richard. *Asceticism in the Graeco-Roman World*. Cambridge: Cambridge University Press, 2009.

Fitzgerald, Allan D., et al., eds. *Augustine through the Ages: An Encyclopedia.* Grand Rapids: Eerdmans, 1999.

Gregory of Tours. *History of the Franks.* Translated by Brehaut Ernest. New York: Columbia University Press, 1916.

Gregory the Great. *The Letters of Gregory the Great, Volume 2: Books 5-9.* Translated by John R. C. Martyn. Toronto: Pontifical Institute for Mediaeval Studies, 2004.

———. *Moral Reflections on the Book of Job, Volume I: Preface to Books 1-5.* Translated by Brian Kerns. Collegeville, MN: Cistercian, 2014.

———. *Pastoral Care.* Translated by Henry Davis. Westminster, MD: Newman, 1950.

Guiver, George. *Company of Voices: Daily Prayer and the People of God.* New York: Pueblo, 1988.

Hadot, Pierre. *Philosophy as a Way of Life.* Malden, MA: Blackwell, 1995.

Hardy, T. J. "The Centrality of the Holy Eucharist." *Theology* 22 (1931) 75-82.

Harkins, Franklin T., and Frans van Liere, eds. *Interpretation of Scripture: Theory—A Selection of Works of Hugh, Andrew, Richard, and Godfrey of St Victor, and of Robert of Melun.* Turnhout, Belgium: Brepols, 2012.

Harrison, Simon. *Augustine's Way into the Will: The Theological and Philosophical Significance of De libero arbitrio.* New York: Oxford University Press, 2006.

Hausherr, Irénée. *Penthos: The Doctrine of Compunction in the Christian East.* Kalamazoo, MI: Cistercian, 1982.

Herbert, George. *The Complete English Poems.* Edited by John Tobin. London: Penguin, 1991.

Hippolytus. *On the Apostolic Tradition.* Translated by Alistair Stewart-Sykes. Crestwood, NY: St. Vladimir's Seminary Press, 2001.

Holloway, Richard, ed. *The Anglican Tradition.* London: Mowbray, 1984.

Hooker, Richard. *Of the Laws of Ecclesiastical Polity, In Two Volumes: Volume One (Books I-IV).* London: Dent, 1907.

Howells, Edward, and Mark McIntosh, eds. *The Oxford Handbook of Mystical Theology.* Oxford: Oxford University Press, 2020.

Janz, Denis R. "Towards a Definition of Late Medieval Augustinianism." *The Thomist* 44.1 (1980) 117-27.

Justin Martyr. *The First and Second Apologies.* Translated by Leslie William Barnard. New York: Paulist, 1997.

Ketley, Joseph, ed. *The Two Liturgies, A.D. 1549, and A.D. 1552: With other Documents Set Forth by Authority in the Reign of King Edward VI.* Cambridge: Cambridge University Press, 1864.

King, Ronald F. "The Origin and Evolution of a Sacramental Formula: *Sacramentum Tantum, Res Et Sacramentum, Res Tantum.*" *The Thomist: A Speculative Quarterly Review* 31 (1967) 21-82.

Knowles, David. *The Monastic Order in England: A History of Its Development from the Times of St. Dunstan to the Fourth Lateran Council 943-1216.* Cambridge: Cambridge University Press, 1950.

Marshall, John S. *Hooker and the Anglican Tradition: An Historical and Theological Study of Hooker's Ecclesiastical Polity.* London: Black, 1963.

McDermott, John M. "The Centrality of the Eucharist." *Antiphon* 25 (2021) 211–44.

Mudge, Bede Thomas. "Monastic Spirituality in Anglicanism." *Review for Religious* 37 (1978) 505–15.

Neil, Bronwen, and Matthew Del Santo, eds. *A Companion to Gregory the Great.* Leiden: Brill, 2013.

Null, Ashley. "Thomas Cranmer and the Anglican Way of Reading Scripture." *Anglican and Episcopal History* 75 (2006) 488–526.

Pascal, Blaise. *Pensées.* Translated by J. A. Krailsheimer. London: Penguin, 1995.

Patton, Kimberley Christine, and John Stratton Hawley, eds. *Holy Tears: Weeping in the Religious Imagination.* Princeton: Princeton University Press, 2005.

Pauley, John-Bede. "The Implication of Monastic Qualities on the Pastoral Provision for the 'Anglican Use.'" *Antiphon* 10.3 (2006) 261–76.

Penner, Jeremy. *Patterns of Daily Prayer in Second Temple Period Judaism.* Leiden: Brill, 2012.

Perkins, William. *A godly and learned exposition of Christs Sermon in the Mount.* Cambridge: Thomas Brooke and Cantrell Legge, 1608.

The Private Devotions of Dr. Lancelot Andrewes, Sometime Lord Bishop of Winchester, Part II. Oxford: James Parker, 1867.

Pusey, Edward Bouverie. *The Holy Eucharist a Comfort to the Penitent.* Oxford: John Henry Parker, 1843.

———. *A Letter to the Right Hon. and Right Rev. the Lord Bishop of London, in Explanation of Some Statements Contained in a Letter by the Rev. W. Dodsworth.* Oxford: John Henry Parker, 1851.

Ross, Kenneth. *Hearing Confessions.* London: SPCK, 1974.

Searle, Mark. "The Journey of Conversion." *Worship* 54 (1980) 35–55.

Sellars, John. *The Art of Living: The Stoics on the Nature and Function of Philosophy.* 2nd ed. London: Bristol Classical, 2009.

Sheldrake, Philip. *A Brief History of Spirituality.* Oxford: Blackwell, 2007.

Shepherd, Massey Hamilton, Jr. *The Oxford American Prayer Book Commentary.* New York: Oxford University Press, 1950.

Sykes, Stephen, and John Booty, eds. *The Study of Anglicanism.* London: SPCK, 1988.

Symonds, R. P. "Deacons in the Early Church." *Theology* 58 (1955) 408–14.

Taft, Robert. *The Liturgy of the Hours in East and West: The Origins of the Divine Office and Its Meaning for Today.* Collegeville, MN: Liturgical, 1986.

Taylor, Jeremy. *Holy Living and Holy Dying, Volume I: Holy Living.* Edited by P. G. Stanwood. Oxford: Clarendon, 1989.

Tebeaux, Elizabeth. "Donne and Hooker on the Nature of Man: The Diverging 'Middle Way.'" *Restoration Quarterly* 24 (1981) 29–44.

Thomas à Kempis. *The Imitation of Christ.* Translated by Leo Sherley-Price. London: Penguin, 1952.

Thornton, Martin. *Pastoral Theology: A Reorientation.* London: SPCK, 1961.

Traherne, Thomas. *Centuries*. Brooklyn, NY: Angelico, 2020.

Trueman, Carl R. *The Rise and Triumph of the Modern Self: Cultural Amnesia, Expressive Individualism, and the Road to Sexual Revolution*. Wheaton, IL: Crossway, 2020.

Vatican II. *Lumen gentium*. Promulgated by Pope Paul VI, November 21, 1964. https://www.vatican.va/archive/hist_councils/ii_vatican_council/documents/vat-ii_const_19641121_lumen-gentium_en.html.

Walton, Izaak. *The lives of Dr. John Donne, Sir Henry Wotton, Mr. Richard Hooker, Mr. George Herbert written by Izaak Walton; to which are added some letters written by Mr. George Herbert, at his being in Cambridge: with others to his mother, the Lady Magdalen Herbert; written by John Donne, afterwards dean of St. Pauls*. London: Tho. Newcomb for Richard Marriott, 1670.

Ware, Kallistos. *The Orthodox Way*. London: Mowbrays, 1979.

Whitlock, Baird W. "The Sacramental Poetry of George Herbert." *South Central Review* 3 (1986) 37–49.

Wilcox, Helen. "Herbert, George (1593–1633), Church of England Clergyman and Poet." *Oxford Dictionary of National Biography*. September 23, 2004; accessed March 7, 2024. https://www.oxforddnb.com/view/10.1093/ref:odnb/9780198614128.001.0001/odnb-9780198614128-e-13025.

William of St. Thierry. *The Works of William of St Thierry: The Golden Epistle—A Letter to the Brethren of Mont Dieu*. Translated by Theodore Berkeley. Kalamazoo, MI: Cistercian, 1980.

Wimbush, Vincent L., and Richard Valantasis, eds. *Asceticism*. Oxford: Oxford University Press, 1998.

Ysebaert, J. *Greek Baptismal Terminology: Its Origins and Early Development*. Nijmegen: Dekker & Van de Vegt N. V., 1962.

Zink, Jesse. "Brief Introductions to Anglican Theology: Christian Mission." *Anglican Theological Review* 104 (2022) 444–62.

Subject Index

Scripture Index

www.ingramcontent.com/pod-product-compliance
Lightning Source LLC
Chambersburg PA
CBHW030848090426
42737CB00009B/1150